SCIENCE AND SECRETS OF THE WHEAT MARKET

IN SIX BOOKS

BURTON HOMER PUG

To understand a science or craft that will produce wealth is one of the most essential achievements of man. Society is so organized that a man does not fully meet the demands of citizenship or satisfy his own ambitions unless he possesses some degree of wealth.

BOOK ONE

THE RIVER OF GOLD

Wheat has been a river of gold flowing down through the history of man ever since he could chip his first idea into imperishable stone or scribble them in half intelligible characters on parchments found in the tombs along the ancient Nile. It is the most fascinating commodity in the world and is today the world's greatest food and its greatest article of commerce. So intimately has it worked its way into the business life of nations that its price is quoted in every important market center on the globe.

The student of these books is doubtless interested in the commercial and speculative features of the wheat market and it is a compliment to his intelligence that he prefers to make his pathway safer and easier by the acquisition of knowledge. The secret of success is in the individual. His willingness to learn of the laws which govern market action and his determination to adjust his own behavior to conform with the art of successful speculation is his passport to financial success.

The grain market has dignity and importance. It is the outgrowth of the country's need for a means of marketing huge grain crops our production of which exceeds that of any other nation on the globe. The grain market is as necessary as railroads, banks or insurance companies. It is a part of our national business organization and has been developed to a point where any individual may participate to whatever extent his finances permit. The business of life is to acquire a competence that life may be lived enjoyed and used to its fullest extent.

3

A COMPLETE COURSE

While this is a complete course in grain trading and most of our leaders are fully acquainted with market terms and market procedure we will refer to a few minor details for those who are yet amateurs in the use of the market.

Grain can be bought or sold on the "futures" market only through brokerage houses. The prospective speculator, intending to buy an option of wheat or other grain, deposits a sum of money with the broker as margin, usually eight to ten cents per bushel, which is for the protection of the broker as well as the individual. A ten cent per bushel margin on five thousand bushels of wheat is $500.00. Some brokers will accept less but it is advisable for safe trading and for the comfort of the trader to use even more than that. Even one thousand dollars would not be too much for a trade of five thousand bushels.

The trader gives his order to the broker to buy five thousand bushels of wheat at whatever price the purchaser decides upon and when the trade is made he receives a confirmation by wire which shows that he is the possessor of five thousand bushels of wheat. Such purchases are called contracts as the buyer can actually demand five thousand bushels of the real wheat when his option month arrives if he chooses to do this. However he can sell out his contract at any time and if he has judged correctly he will have a profit on it and will receive that profit from the broker when the trade is closed.

Trades can be made in any size or quantity from one thousand bushels to a million or more. Small lots less than five thousand are called job lots and are usually traded in by small operators.
The Chicago Board of Trade is the largest futures market in the United States or in the world. Other markets are at Kansas City, St. Louis, Minneapolis and Duluth. The two most noted foreign markets are at Liverpool and Buenos Aires.

YOU AND YOUR BROKER

The broker is a very important individual in your market business but it is well not to get on such intimate terms that he feels himself to be your needed advisor. Be decisive and dominant in your own course because you are making a study of the market while few others do. Your broker wants you to succeed. He enjoys your success with you. Few men are so hard-boiled that they can see a client lose with complacence. When you win, your broker will share your pleasure. In some way he feels that he is a part of your success but intimacy with the broker is likely to invite carelessness. The trader is inclined to accept the broker's opinion rather than to study out for himself the logical action of the market. Self-confidence is an indispensable asset to the trader and he gains self-confidence by making an earnest study of the market just as the reader is doing now. No trader can afford to sacrifice his self-confidence or the knowledge that he gains to his broker or to anyone else. It is his stock in trade, his secret, his method and it should be kept from curious eyes and curious minds. This brings us to another heading as noted below.

THREE REQUISITES

Whether the speculator be a beginner or an experienced operator there are three things which will loom very large in his financial success. They are:

DETERMINATION, INDUSTRY, SECRECY

The business of speculation is ample and is fascinating. It will merit the full and complete effort of anyone. Therefore, it is well that the trader should personally resolve to enter the speculative field with determination and earnestness. In no branch of business life will thoroughness pay like it does in the grain market. Your money is good, hard American dollars earned by dint of hard work and saving and it should not be subjected to waste by haphazard trading. Your money will work for you as nothing else can but it must be given intelligent personal assistance and this requires study.

Go into the business of speculation with as much thoroughness as you would go into surgery or into the practice of law. Speculation is not a simple game of chance for the amusement of the trader but a deep, scientific study that will require your keenest intelligence and will pay the student in proportion to his knowledge of its laws.

INDUSTRY has no substitute. Any plan for making money is a matter of work and study and the market is not an exception. Fortunately the study of market action carries with it a deep fascination. There is real pleasure in the study of any plan or process which makes money but for intense interest, the market outstrips all others. Market laws are not difficult to understand, but they are constantly before you in these perpetually moving markets, and to understand the fluctuations you must understand the laws which cause them, and that is a simple matter of industry, of studiousness, but your study of the market will be a joyful task because you are preparing to harness it to fulfill your needs.

SECRECY in your market operations is a virtue that yields excellent returns. It is a strange fact that when you disclose your personal plans to others you disperse your power and scatter your effort. You unconsciously lose something which cannot be recovered. You divide your cherished possession with someone else who probably cares nothing for it. Once you let others in on what you are intending to do, your own interest seems to lag. You lack that driving power that remains yours so long as your cherished aim is a secret. When Edison was perfecting some of his famous inventions he scarcely left his workshop and he slept only when nature drove him to sleep but when he came out he had something that astonished the world. Your prosperity cannot be hidden. Let your success speak for itself and if, perchance, you make mistakes as you are bound to do at times you will feel a deep satisfaction in knowing the secret is yours. You can resume your operations with greater assurance and accuracy because you have no critics to condemn you. It is the habit of people—even your friends—to minimize your successes and to exaggerate your errors. Therefore, the less they know of your personal plans the better your chance for future success.

Determination, industry and secrecy are matters of personal culture and are highly important to successful market operations. Particular stress has been placed on these personal market habits because the action of the market, into which we are now about to go, is very largely made up of traders' habits, not of their reasoning, and in so far as the student increases his knowledge, thus far will he excel the average trader. A correct knowledge of the market is to a large degree a correct knowledge of the psychology of the trading public.

THE CROWD AND THE INDIVIDUAL

The masses trade wrongly because they do not observe the three requisites mentioned in the previous paragraph. The majority of traders try to follow some other trader or some market authority because they do not take the time to learn about the market for themselves. Thinking is not an easy task. Most men prefer to make a guess at the market rather than engage in the effort of studying but to imitate others is to become a parrot and eventually you will make nothing and will lose all. Practice with study is the formula that has made our big speculators, our captains of industry and our financial wizards.

In the market the crowd is wrong ninety per cent of the time because it fails to think. The individual who thinks is immediately different from the crowd. If the trader would avoid the losing habit of following the crowd he should do just what the reader is doing now study the market. Study brings ideas and ideas are the most potent powers in the world. Mental effort is the energy which you use in climbing the mountain at the top of which stands financial success. Study is shunned by the crowd, yet every great book, every useful invention and every great structure is the direct product of thought. The reader has already designated himself as different from the crowd because he is making a careful study of the market wherein may rest his financial future.

7

The more deeply you are interested in the market the better you will like the six books in this course because they will take you through the whole range of market action pointing out the causes or big movements and how to anticipate them. The people as a mass will not go to this trouble therefore, the student has a tremendous advantage over the unthinking trader. He gets the money which the careless trader loses. It is not meant that the study of the market is difficult. Quite the opposite is true. The scientist is devoted to his laboratory, the writer to his library and the market student will be just as intensely interested in delving into the secrets of our great financial institution, the grain market.

MANIPULATION

Manipulation, as it is known in the grain market, is not so prevalent as of former years because the wheat market has become a world affair and a few individuals cannot control it as they used to twenty or thirty years ago when such events as the "Leiter Corner" occurred. However, in big bull markets there is still some manipulation. It is usually a concentrated buying campaign staged by individuals with ample finances who force the market upward by purchasing on all small reactions. The market is thus supported and its rapid upward course invites traders from all walks of life. When these operators believe the market cannot go higher they sell out and let "the public" have the wheat. Of course, when the big fellows are through the market goes down. These big markets are not all the result of manipulation. Often it happens that spells of weather, hot as the breath of Sahara, shoot across the fields and destroy corn or wheat by the millions of bushels daily. During such spells the public is readily induced to buy wheat or corn. Manipulators are not always successful. Sometimes they devote much effort to advancing a market only to find that they cannot stimulate the public interest. They have to sell out and often at a loss. Manipulation is present in bull markets but seldom in a bear market. The public follows readily in a bull movement because it prefers advancing prices, but a bear market is against public sentiment and destroys leadership.

USING MARKET MOVEMENTS

All barter and sale of merchandise is based upon fluctuation in price. These fluctuations have developed enormously in the grain markets and in the stock market because of the volume of trading therein. We have big swings, small swings and daily movements all scattered along through the market in promiscous profusion. Some of these movements are entirely out of proportion and should be avoided because there is no possible method of forecasting them. The failure of traders at the brokerage house is in trying to follow these unforecastable movements. They become habituated to "in and out trading" and fall back upon the simple and easy act of guessing from which there is no possible success. Loss attends with certainty the efforts of the small trader who plays for the daily movement. Some very excellent swings can be forecasted and the student is shown how this may be done farther on in this course.

A daily forecasting service is obliged to comply with a very large and urgent demand for forecasts of the daily action before the day begins. A majority of those using the market, including the millers who buy wheat and hedge it or who are selling flour, constantly try to profit by the small movements; therefore, the need for knowing the daily action is highly important. Unfortunately the daily action is almost unforecastable. If a Service Letter correctly foretells the daily action sixty per cent of the time it is doing well, but the speculator who is entering the market for positive results on an increasing scale and who intends to stay with the game until he wins should plan his financial future on the big movements which operate under definite market laws, for in these only is ultimate success. Whenever you find a man who has lost money in the market you will find he was either trading on the small fluctuations or was playing for long pull without knowing the laws of the market which govern these long pull movements. When the student acquaints himself with the few powerful laws on which the entire market is based he will then understand many of the small movements which formerly were a puzzle to him. Learn the laws and habits of the market and the balance is easy.

Big surges occur in the market often without apparent cause. Orders come into the Chicago Board of Trade or into the other Exchanges from all parts of the country by telegraph. At times there will be a heavy wave of buying orders and the price will rise rapidly. At other times a rush of selling orders, without apparent cause will arrive and the market breaks. These are chance happenings and are quickly corrected by the laws which govern the main trend. Crop news is the most prolific of results in grain movements; in fact, nearly all big movements in grains are brought about by a shortage or a surplus of crops. Weather changes quickly and produces heavy loss by drought or hot winds in a very short time. This accounts for the predominance of short term bull movements which, later in this course, are described as the "six weeks bull movements," a type of action occurring almost every year and very prolific of profits.

LIQUIDATION

Liquidation means selling out long grain. The term is also applied to other things in a broad sense such as the liquidation of the bond market, the stock market or of cotton. Even the livestock market has its waves of liquidation such as occurred in June, 1932, when hogs sold at $2.85, the lowest price on record. Liquidation in the speculative market is brought about by heavy crop prospects or by some event which causes traders to believe they cannot realize profits on their long grain. A specific cause of liquidation is the habitual use of narrow margins or in other words the habit of overtrading. Large operators, who have access to the books of brokers, frequently discover the fact that a large amount of wheat is being held by traders on a thin margin and take advantage of them by forcing the market down until these weekly margined accounts are obliged to sell out at a loss. The talented operators buy up this grain that is being liquidated and having secured it at a low price will then stimulate an advance and harvest astonishing profits. This driving out of weak accounts is called forced liquidation.

GRAINS OR STOCKS, WHICH?

Trading must suit the taste of the man trading. If he is more familiar with grains he will do his best work in the grain market. In a grain country where the farmer, the miller and the merchant are all interested in the prosperity of wheat and corn the largest amount of public interest will develop in the grains. In eastern sections of the country where manufacturing has a wider development and where financial institutions are more prominent the mass of public traders is more intensely interested in the stock market. However, there are times when a bull market in wheat becomes so impressive that it invites countrywide participation and traders will send in orders for wheat from every corner of the country from the Atlantic to the Pacific. In the long run the trader should follow that which suits his taste as he will be the most successful in the field he likes best.

In 1932 the price of New York stocks by the midyear had dropped down so low that the public all but abandoned the stock market. People were afraid to invest, and they saw no profit in speculation. The volume of stocks went down to a few hundred thousand shares daily. The public quickly turns away from a dull market. Activity or fluctuation in prices is the sole means of deriving a profit and if a market goes "stale" the public deserts it.

Wheat is the favorite speculative commodity because its periods of quiet are always brief. From every dull period—which seldom lasts more than thirty days—wheat emerges into sharp activity. It seldom disappoints the trader long. Speculation in wheat occurs in every big market on the globe and being connected with telegraphic cables each market knows what the others are doing and all within the space of a few minutes' time. Commissions vary in the different countries and sometimes in the same country. For instance, the commission for five thousand bushels of wheat in Chicago is $12.50 while in Kansas City it is $10. The amateur trader should learn the details of trading by a visit to his broker where he can better acquire detailed information than he could by reading it on the pages of this book.

11

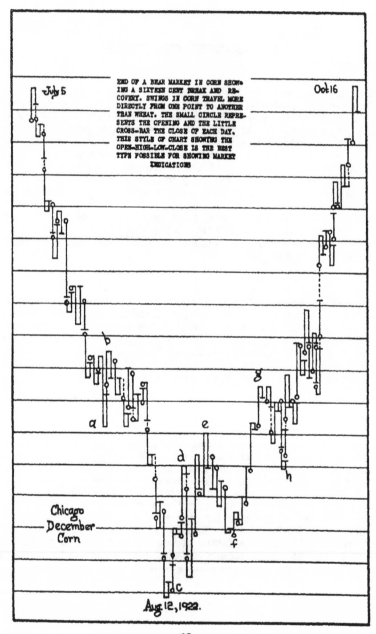

July 5

END OF A BEAR MARKET IN CORN SHOW-
ING A SIXTEEN CENT BREAK AND RE-
COVERY. SWINGS IN CORN TRAVEL MORE
DIRECTLY FROM ONE POINT TO ANOTHER
THAN WHEAT. THE SMALL CIRCLE REPRE-
SENTS THE OPENING AND THE LITTLE
CROSS-BAR THE CLOSE OF EACH DAY.
THIS STYLE OF CHART SHOWING THE
OPEN-HIGH-LOW-CLOSE IS THE BEST
TYPE POSSIBLE FOR SHOWING MARKET
INDICATIONS

Oct 16

b

a

g

e

d

h

Chicago
December
Corn

f

c

Aug. 12, 1922.

WHEAT THE LEADER

Of the four principal grains wheat is preeminently the leader, corn comes next, then oats and lastly rye. Nearly all grains follow wheat in some measure but more especially during the winter months after the crop season is over. Wheat should be given the most study; in fact, it should be used in speculative trading almost to the exclusion of other grains. There are occasional times when corn develops a bull movement independently of wheat such as happened in 1930, then it is wise to step into the corn market and take whatever profit it will yield. A bull market in corn is more rapid and direct than in wheat and does not follow other market habits quite so well as wheat but can nevertheless be readily used by the speculator for very excellent profits.

Rye is well known as a "tricky" grain. It often does what is least expected and it is the author's judgment that it should be avoided at all times. This country produces around forty million bushels of rye annually and the amount of trading in rye futures is very small. The action of the rye market based upon the market habits of only a few traders and the movements in this grain are therefore unreliable and have not the advantage of the mass opinion expressed in the movements of wheat.

Oats was once a popular grain and was traded in heavily because of its low price but the use of farm tractors and the tremendous reduction in the use of horses has worked against this grain. The movements have become so small that little profit is available. It is the author's opinion that it will be difficult for oats to come back into favor because the farms will use horses only under the most severe periods of a depression. Power driven farm machinery far excels horses and it is doubtful if the farms will take a backward step by returning to the use of horse drawn machinery.

Since the small trader can trade in wheat in lots as small as one thousand bushels and the larger trader can deal in the grain in lots of a million or more it would seem a matter of simple judgment that wheat should be adopted as the most satisfactory grain for speculation.

MAKING CHARTS

Charting the movements of the grain options is an absolute necessity for successfully operating in the market. Some students keep charts very accurately but most people fail to take charting seriously and do not keep their options up. Some use a simple line for the high and low. This type we do not favor as it does not permit the forming of certain very important angles that are highly useful in forecasting.

On page 12 you will find the style of chart which the author prefers and which he uses in all commodities and stocks. This is a chart of a break in corn and a prompt recovery. The break from July 5 to August 12 is what we term a **vertical break** and it has a very important meaning which you will learn when you get to Book Four where vertical breaks are discussed. The main object in this particular chart is to show that the open, high, low and close of each daily movement may be clearly shown and that it gives a clearer picture of the market than the usual straight, perpendicular line, showing the high and low. There is much prejudice against the use of charts but it is mostly by people who will not take the trouble to make them or keep them up. Of recent years since such a large number of our population has been trading in stocks and grains the use of charts by individuals, financial papers and financial institutions has been greatly increased. Government Departments at Washington use charts and graphs for every imaginable purpose. In an editorial of the Saturday Evening Post of July 11, 1931, this statement will be noted:

> "We believe that millions of people would find valuable educational material in one of those familiar charts which show business fluctuation. The general effect of such a chart on the beholder is somewhat like that of a relief map. Students find that there is a wide variety in the characteristics and combinations of different periods."

The public is becoming educated to the use of charts just as it is to other new things such as the radio or iceless refrigeration.

ORIGIN OF MARKET LAWS

Market movements assemble themselves into a few conspicuous types of action that have a certain orderliness which may be regarded as of sufficient frequency to be governed by laws. Close analysis discloses the fact that market laws have their origin in human trading habits. The one unchangeable fact of the business of life is **human nature.** To get at the heart of the market we must get at the heart of man. The best indications of future market action are obtained by coming directly to the market itself which is a sort of solidified or crystallized form of human hopes and needs sometimes termed the "psychology of the market."

No firmer foundation could be found for market laws since whatever variations are brought into our civilization by a developing race the basic or ancient elements of human behavior remain always the same. Fear, hope and greed remain steadfastly the driving forces that make men do what they do. When the daily action of a market is charted it becomes a picture of these most powerful human habits. Even the physical laws of Nature are not much more stable than these laws of human conduct which, in the bartering and selling of grains, become market laws.

BULL MARKETS register an abounding enthusiasm in the belief that prices should be higher and are going higher and that profits can be derived from purchasing grain.

BEAR MARKETS are the bursted bubbles of bull markets. They represent disappointment and pessimism under the belief that the bull market was carried too high and that prices must come down. The bull and bear markets contain all of the important elements of market action. The smaller movements are but component parts of these two types of action. When a bull market ends, a bear market sets in immediately. When a bear market is finished and liquidation is complete then the small, slow beginnings of the next bull market get under way. The bull market usually starts slowly. The bear market always starts with sharp action.

15

To achieve success market laws must be obeyed just as we must obey civil laws if we would be successful in citizenship or just as we must obey natural laws if we would be successful in the laboratory. When we disobey laws we suffer. In the market we pay for our ignorance of its laws by the loss of money. Few people understand the laws of market action and some even attempt to deny that they exist. This is one of the reasons why only a few are ultimately successful in trading.

TRADING HABITS AND MARKET HABITS

Price movements are mostly based upon fundamentals. In the grain market the chief fundamental is **crop outlook**. In the stock market the chief fundamental is business outlook. The wide public, in making its market deals, falls into natural human habits and these in turn become market habits but the smaller actions and habits are not of sufficient importance to be termed laws. Your neighbor or your friend or yourself, upon reading the news about wheat, will be inclined to take certain action, but not everybody interprets the market the same; hence one buys wheat while the other sells. The result is the erratic movements that so often disconcert the trader.

Brushing aside the smaller surface habits we may strip the human being down to three powerful mental forces which are as permanent as the race itself:

GREED (covetousness). Nothing bad or base but an urgent desire to get all we can as fast as we can because the Almighty has allotted to us but a brief span of life in which to enjoy what we earn.

HOPE (desire). The wish for better things, for home comforts, for education, travel and the accumulation of reserves that will guarantee security for those who are dependent upon us.

FEAR (terror of poverty). A biting concern lest the money or possessions we already have and are risking may be snatched away from us and cripple our ability to earn more in the future.

16

Every important movement in the market is the direct result of one or more of these human impulses. Sometimes a majority of those trading fall into unison as to opinion of the market and straightway the price moves persistently in one direction. Thus we have the bull market. Basic laws of the market are few because the basic laws of human nature are few.

MARKET RULES in large numbers have been developed by students but a plethora of rules is confusing. Only the more powerful impulses in human nature run uniform therefore only a very few market rules will be accurate. It is these most important rules that will be used in these books and it will be found that all conditions and movements are fully covered by them. Certain writers have developed as many as forty or even a hundred "market rules" in an attempt to cover the smaller erratic movements. Experience will quickly teach the user of these promiscous rules that they are futile and misleading. They "work" once in awhile and lose money for the trader the balance of the time.

Rules that are worth using are so definite that most of them may be termed market laws. Yet they are usually in the form of rules and may be applied when the charted action of the market shows they should be used. After issuing a daily grain letter for over eight years (without missing a market day) the author has come to the conclusion that:

Most of the daily movements cannot be forecasted.

Trading on daily movements is very popular.

Waiting patiently for big swings is very profitable.

The best profits are made by following a bull move.

Second best profits made by following a bear move.

Professional grain speculators do not attempt to use the daily movements. The popular practice with them is to wait for a bull market situation to arise when the price is low and crop damage appearing. Then they "hit hard." They drive a market through to the finish, then reverse their position and follow the bear market down.

"FOLLOW THROUGH"

Lloyd George in making a speech before an American audience, declared that the most vital plan for an individual or for a nation, when once a policy was adopted, was to "follow through." It is especially true of the market. Making business is the biggest business of life. If the grain market is used to further one's financial plans one should learn to use it correctly or else abandon it entirely.

The stock market and the grain market are the nation's two greatest financial institutions. Smart men are operating in them for profit. The successful trader must master the market or learn the art of following the footsteps of master operators.

BUT STICK TO YOUR JOB or your profession and make grain trading your side line. It may become the most important thing in your life but in the early stages of market experience the trader should use the market with care studying its habits and laws and keeping to his regular occupation as a sort of refuge or support. It will give you a dignity and self-confidence very useful in your life as a citizen and will help balance your judgment in your market operations. Brokers frankly admit that merchants who do not visit the exchange but who make their market deals by telephone are the most successful.

One of the most successful traders in the author's knowledge is a man who lives in a town which has no "exchange" or wire house. All of his work is done over the telephone. He maintains a large mercantile business and deals in large quantities of grain—when he believes conditions are right. He has a radio in his office from which he receives quotations every 15 minutes. He is an eager student of market action, having bought a "Grain Market Study Course" issued a few years ago (by the present author) and being aware of certain types of pivotal movements he plays these movements hard. Small movements do not interest him or worry him. He is a "big game" hunter.

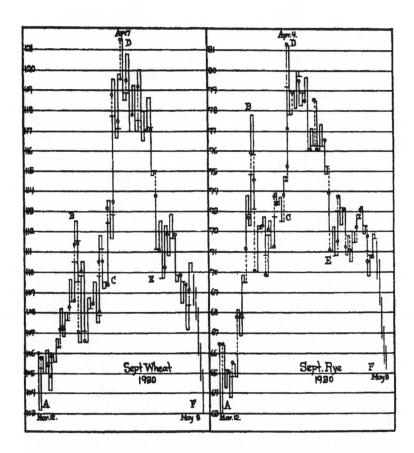

WHEAT, in its market activities, is the most rapid of all grains and being subject to severe weather damage frequently develops bull movements. Since 1922 eleven bull movements have occurred, ranging from 23 cents to $1.00 in extent. A normal crop for the United States is 850 million bushels and for the world 3,500 million bushels is about the required amount. A reduction of a few hundred millions from the world supply always causes a bull move in all markets. Other grains largely—though not always—follow the movements of wheat. During 1930 a 35 cent bull movement occurred in corn and only a small flurry in wheat.

RYE gains most of its importance because of a foreign demand by countries who use rye bread, Germany, Austria and Scandanavia particularly. The U. S. produces annually about 40-50 million bushels. The market action of rye is similar to that of wheat, but the heavy volume of trading in wheat makes wheat superior.

19

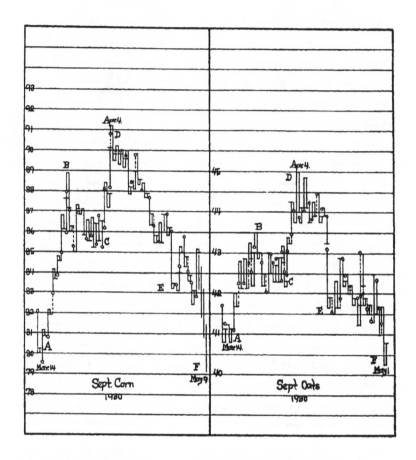

CORN is second in importance as a speculative grain; also as a matter of farm prosperity although during some years it adds more prosperity to the farms than wheat owing to its use as feed for livestock. In the heavy corn states corn is a speculative favorite. We produce normally about three billions of bushels per annum and use 80 per cent of the grain at home. Corn follows wheat in its market action except during years of severe crop damage.

OATS is the smallest in price of the grains, yet it has its swings and its bull and bear movements almost as regularly as the other grains. It follows wheat more closely than it follows corn. A normal crop is about 1,250 million bushels. The adoption of power machinery on farms instead of using horses is greatly reducing the use of oats.

Comparing the daily movements of the four grains, shown on pages 19 and 20, it will be seen that each grain has certain individual action, slightly different from the others. It is the author's judgment that the ambitious trader should devote his attention to wheat but not to adhere to this grain so closely as to prevent his taking advantage of periods when great weather damage occurs to other crops. For instance, in 1930 the country had a good wheat crop but hot weather in July and August cut the corn crop several hundred million bushels. This, naturally, produced a bull movement in corn. Such movements should be utilized to the limit by the trader because it is these powerful movements that make the big profits and make them quickly.

Millers and grain dealers have to keep up on oats, corn and rye because they are dealing in these grains and they will wish to sell hedges against grain purchased and will later wish to know the most favorable place to lift these hedges. By watching the wheat options they will be able to forecast many of the best movements in corn and the other grains, but all through this course examples are shown of the four chief grains so the trader or grain dealer may learn the habits of action for each grain.

Corn, for example, when moving from a low position to a high position, makes its way much more directly and with fewer reactions than wheat. Declines in corn are likewise rather abrupt and with few rallies. Note the action of corn in the chart on page 12. The daily volume of trading may be cited for one day during a very active market to show the proportion for each grain. On July 18, 1929, a very active day in the grain markets, the volume for the four grains was as follows:

Total volume for wheat..............139,108,000 Bushels

Total volume for corn .... 31,129,000 Bushels

Total volume for oats............... 11,354,000 Bushels

Total volume for rye .... 3,356,000 Bushels

21

USING THE BIG SWINGS

The failure of many people to achieve success in the market is because they fall into the fatal habit of trading in-and-out on the daily movements. This practice is common at the brokerage houses where men watch the board constantly. They become fascinated by the ever changing quotations and invariably digress into the "In-And-Out" habit that leads to failure. They try to play both sides of the market, an utter impossibility for the keenest mind. Later in this course the student will be given a method for in-and-out trading, which is followed persistently by the major trend. This plan of trading, followed correctly, can be made eminently successful because it follows one trend only. No system known to the author can follow the wheat market through its minor ups and downs. Big swings may be utilized with excellent profits but they should be followed by means of the methods taught in Book Four. The author has subscribers to the Daily Service who make excellent profits on these big swings.

NATURAL BULLS AND NATURAL BEARS

Some men prefer to trade only on the long side. The short side is against their taste and confuses them. Such persons are termed Natural Bulls. Conversely, there are other traders of a temperament that prefers the down side. It may have happened that their best market deals have chanced to be short sales and they fall into the belief that the short side is best fitted to their makeup. They are constantly on the lookout for a rally on which to sell short. These traders are Natural Bears. The most fortunate person is he who takes an impersonal view of the market and who can adjust himself to follow either side, knowing that market laws for advances are no stronger than the market laws for declines. Such traders can follow a bull market through, then turn squarely about and follow the bear market back to its origin. In the stock market it is estimated that ninety per cent of the trading public prefers the long side. In the grain market it is probable that eighty per cent prefer the long side. It may be added that professional traders use both sides of the market.

22

Taking the mass of traders the country over, they are predominantly bullish. Almost every man has property of some kind, or a business which is better off when prices advance. It is natural, therefore, that the majority of men are anxious to see advancing prices, and in making their market deals they take the long side.

BROKERS

Most of the brokerage houses are reasonably safe for the entrusting of your funds. The older houses that have weathered financial storms of the past are usually the best. When the trader is preparing to enter the market and has no established brokerage connection he should watch the newspapers for the houses that advertise the most freely, as consistent advertising is one of the signs of a progressive broker. It is well to become personally acquainted with your broker and establish a business friendship which will promote harmony in market deals. The broker is entirely human and wishes his clients to succeed. He may be a busy man but he will take time off to advise favored clients of special wire news that may come in. However, it is wise to avoid the brokerage house after you have established your "contact" with the broker. A broker friend of the author recently made the statement that his most prosperous customer was a gentleman of some 70 years who had retired from a mercantile business and was engaged in buying and selling stocks. He bought his stocks outright to avoid interest charges and the dangers of margin accounts and thus at one stroke he eliminated the faulty habit of overtrading. He traded in moderate lots, although his ample means would have permitted him to trade in shares by the thousands. He seldom appeared at the brokerage house except for the purpose of delivering certain shares, which he had sold out, or for other detail business with the broker, and it was noticed that he seldom cast so much as a glance at the quotation board. He acknowledged to the broker that his percentage of profits on his comparatively small stock deals was much greater than the profits he derived from his mercantile business before he retired. The chief virtue in his market policy was that he avoided overtrading.

OFFERS AND BIDS

This form of trading in futures is also termed puts and calls, privileges and grain insurance. Fifteen minutes after the close of the regular grain market the market for privileges opens. Brokers make deals for clients as in regular futures. Offers or calls are above the market. They can be bought on "tomorrow," for "this week" or for "next week," meaning that they are good for that length of time. They can be either bought or sold. In case they are sold the seller gets a net profit of about $4.50 for 5,000 bushels. If the trader should buy offers for "today" on 5,000 bushels of wheat at one cent above the close they would cost him about $8.75 figuring the new tax assessed by congress in 1932 (former price $6.25). If the price during the day goes up through the offers and closes above them he becomes owner of 5,000 bushels of long wheat which he will have to margin or dispose of at once. If the price fails to go above the offers the trader loses the $7.25 paid for the offers. In case the price runs up through the offers and then closes down below them he still loses the cost of the offers.

If the reader should buy bids for "today" he would pay $5.50 for them, as no tax was placed upon bids since they are supposed to have a bullish effect upon the market. If the price closes below the bid price the buyer owns 5,000 bushels of short wheat and will have to margin or close it out. If the market closes above the bid price the trader loses the cost of the bids—$5.50.

If the price goes through the offers or bids by 3/8 cent or more the trader can take profits on his grain, but it requires the first 1/4 cent through to pay the commission. If bids are sold and the price closed below the bid price that makes the trader long of wheat. Large traders often get long in this way when they believe wheat is about to advance. If offers are sold and the price closes above the offer price then the trader has short wheat. This is often practiced by traders who expect a break in the market.

24

BIDS are very useful in a bull market as the trader can use them to buy against. That is he can buy bids when he anticipates a reaction that would enable him to buy wheat at a favorable figure. For instance, he might have 20,000 bushels of long wheat properly margined and wish to take on more with a minimum of risk. He could buy bids on 20,000 and when the price drops close to the bid price he can buy 20,000 bushels. If the price turns and goes up he has that much extra wheat or 40,000 total. If the price goes through the bids he simply closes out the new lot of wheat against the bids and suffers a very small loss. Heavy traders use this plan successfully.

Offers or bids also serve as "insurance" against loss. For instance, if long, the trader can buy bids as protection and in case of a break he will lose only the difference between the closing price and the bid price. Should the trader have short wheat he can insure himself against excessive loss by purchasing offers. In case of a sharp or unexpected rise he loses only the difference between the closing price and the offers.

Next week's bids also this week's bids, are traded in to a considerable extent, usually by those who believe that the market is about to undergo a sharp break. Next week's offers and this week's offers may be bought in the same way.
It is the author's opinion that most of this trading in offers and bids is money lost except when offers are used to protect short sales in a bear market or when bids are used to buy against in a bull market.

The best way to acquire information about offers and bids is to make a deal in them and talk to your broker about the details. They appear puzzling but are really quite simple when fully understood. If the reader of these lines will write to Logan and Bryan of Chicago or of Winnipeg they can get a small booklet, free, covering this subject more fully than we have space to devote to it here. Traders near Kansas City can get a free booklet from B. C. Christopher and Company, Board of Trade Building, describing the use of offers and bids.

DECEPTIVE "INDICATIONS"

Amongst local traders and at the exchanges are often heard market adages and "old traders' rules" that are passed about and often, unfortunately, acted upon. Such phrases as "Thursday for bulls and Friday for bears," "break seven, break eleven," meaning that in case the market breaks seven cents it will break farther to eleven, are common amongst the trading fraternity. Certain traders fancy the market will turn at a given time of day, say eleven-thirty and make trades in anticipation of such turns. Some claim the ninth, nineteenth and twenty-ninth days are important, but we suspect the rhyme of the numbers has more to do with it than the dates. Using these small rules is about as effective for trading as using bread pills would be for curing typhoid fever. It is well to view any of the market catch phrases with suspicion. They reflect the desire of the small trader to catch the small movements for which there is little hope and which movements have no definite rule of action.

A widely spread fallacy is found in a tabloid set of rules named "A Voice from the Tomb" (evidently a dead one) which have found their way into market literature. These rules are also called "calendar dates," meaning the calendar dates on which to buy or sell grain: They are quoted here as a sample of rules which are utterly useless:

Sell wheat....... Jan. 10th	Buy corn .... March 1st
Buy wheat ..... Feb. 22nd	Sell corn .... May 20th
Sell wheat ...... May 10th	Buy corn.. ... June 25th
Buy wheat . ... July 1st	Sell corn .. Aug. 10th
Sell wheat ..... Sept. 10th	Investigation has proven
Buy wheat .. .. .Nov. 28th	these dates are worthless.

A few simple rules suggested by a professional trader who made a fortune on using practical methods and personal judgment are herewith quoted. However, the student should be satisfied only with a personal knowledge of market laws acquired by his own study. Judgment should be backed with actual knowledge.

Broad rules suggested by a professional trader:

"Never trust to luck and try to guess the market. Base your trades and risk your money only upon intelligent forecasts and information."

"A bull market begins when everything is darkest and the financial columns of papers are devoted to bad news in general."

"Let your watchword be large margins. Never trade in lots you cannot margin ten to twenty cents."

"Wait for keen definite action and clear indications and don't attempt to trade every day."

The most vital and decisive indications are found in the charted actions of the grains. From the most impressive movements laws of action are devised and the purpose of his course is to teach the profitable use of these market laws.

EXAMPLE OF MANIPULATED MARKET

On page 28 will be found a charted wheat movement that may be said to have been largely manipulated. That is, professional traders being aware that the public was anxious to see wheat prices higher and having dry seeding conditions in the southwest to help, they considered it feasible to attempt a buying campaign in wheat. Congress always does its "probing" and "investigating" of market operations when prices are down. There is no criticism of any individual or group who helps put prices up. For this reason traders felt some reassurance and safety in attempting to stimulate a buying wave in wheat. It succeeded well. The actual events and conditions surrounding the market during that movement are given on a succeeding page to show how the price movement can go against conditions at certain times and that public sentiment is the most powerful of all market factors.

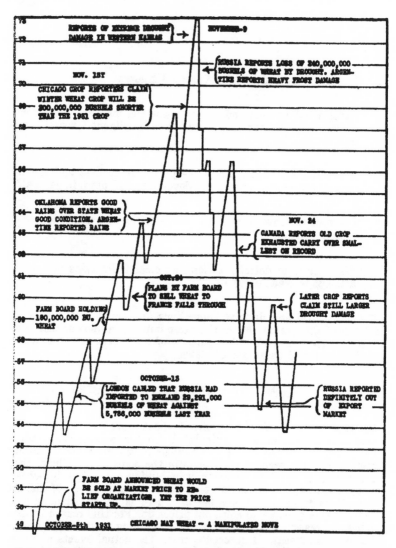

The above outlined chart shows a small bull movement in May wheat which occurred in the fall of 1931. Skilled operators were in this market and, as usual, had the very excellent help of a large number of small traders who entered the movement as soon as the professionals had it started well on the way. The object of this particular chart is to show that the advance took place during much bearish news and that after the top was made the decline occurred during very bullish news. Thus we must infer tnat this movement was manipulated.

Manipulated movements are not necessarily evil or wrong as they add new and justified value to grains. The market is caught up out of a paralyzing rut by intelligent men who, believing the price is too low, have the judgment and finances to put prices higher.

At the time of this writing the price of wheat is at the lowest in fifty years, viz. 44 to 45 cents per bushel for July wheat. (July-1932). At the extreme low price prevailing the best thing that could happen to wheat and to the farmer would be for speculators to pick up the market and give it a bull movement. Naturally they would use the newspapers and wire bulletins to influence the public to buy, an entirely worthy step as conditions must be advertised to convince people. Otherwise they would stand idle and allow the wheat price to remain unjustly low. These operators would eventually draw a good following into the market and in the strict sense of the word it would be a manipulated movement but the good would be incalculable.

There should be no criticism of men who have the judgment, finances and courage to stimulate higher prices when conditions justify them. Few bull movements are started except from low prices and with weather conditions adverse to the crop. Most harm arising from bull market operations is from over extended advances caused by inordinate and ungoverned buying on the part of the public.

Yet regardless of unrestrained public participation which seems to run away with the market at times, these bull movements conform remarkably well with staid market laws and phenomena of which you will learn more as you proceed in this course. No bull movement occurs but what is in accord with established market laws. Tops can be forecasted, and breaks confirmed in all types of bull movements no matter how erratic they may appear. The reason is because market laws are the products of human nature which remain steady and are consistently the same from generation to generation. The bull market of 1922 is similar to that of 1927 or 1929. One generation of traders passes away but in the next generation the market performs the same old way.

START LITTLE — GROW BIG

Even though the ambitious trader may have ample capital it is a wise policy to conserve his funds and start building up his resources by small trades, increasing as his earned revenue increases. The market, when used correctly, returns money at an amazing rate. Its beneficence should not be tested, or dared or misused. Stories are often related of men who started on a "shoestring" and ran it up into a fortune, but these incidents are few. More money is lost in trying to run a small sum of money up to a big sum than was ever acquired by the shoestring method. For the amateur trader with modest funds it is well to start on a small sum and build it up with the greatest care until his funds begin to justify larger deals. After that there should be no variation from the policy of trading safely. By trading safely is meant that the market be followed according to its laws as taught in this course and by absolutely refusing to overtrade. When one has been successful for awhile it becomes a matter of self mastery to prevent indulging too heavily. In fact success in any endeavor entails one with a greater need of personal culture and self control.

A young engineer of the author's acquaintance became interested in the wheat market because he heard others were making money therein. Without experience he started in but having a technical education found it easy to chart and follow the grain. However it was a long bull market he was in and had all of the advantages of a one way market. Starting with $250 he eventually increased it to the astonishing sum of $80,000 and in a comparatively short time. He felt a bit self confident over the fact and entertaining the idea that he knew all about the market, set out to make a quick fortune. The first big deal he made lost him $20,000. It was an eyeopener. His good judgment prevailed. From his remaining $60,000 he drew enough to buy a nice home, took a lot on each side of the house and placing a neat balance in liberty bonds, he came back to the market with $10,000 intending, quite sensibly, to make his way more slowly. His big battle was with himself and he won.

WHAT ARE FUNDAMENTALS?

In the wheat market fundamentals refer chiefly to crop conditions and supply of grain on hands. Export demand is important as a fundamental but this follows a short crop or is increased by a short crop. Visible supply, car receipts, premiums and other statistics naturally depend on crop conditions so the trader can disregard all of the lesser factors affecting the market and devote his study to the crop condition and to the supply on hand as the chief inspiring causes of market movements.

But it must be understood that the fundamentals are the cause of long bull movements. Numberless smaller movements may take place, many of them directly opposite to the real trend, while the price is engaged in making a long move. It is the judgment of the author that the trader need not concern himself with even the chief fundamentals except in times of great stress in crops such as a severe drought or hot winds on the growing grain. It is better to let the market interpret the conditions rather than expect conditions to forecast the market. The element of human opinion constantly modifies the fundamentals. Some believe the weather is doing much damage while others think the damage small. Market action solves the problem, hence we urge the student to devote his study to market laws, putting crops and conditions secondary.

KEEP BOOKS

It is well to keep a careful record of all transactions showing the purchase price and selling price, commissions and tax deductions. Thus you have a ready account to check up with the brokerage house statement and to keep yourself posted on your operations. When correctly followed the market should show a very consistent increase in your revenues. Occasional losses will be expected but in the course of months you should be steadily forging ahead. If not you should take measure of yourself to see what you are doing that is not right. Life is too short to waste it in frivolous trading. Make it count. The smallest amount you can trade in (1,000 bushels) will, if used correctly with ample margin, make an astonishing profit. If you are a heavy trader using large sums of money it will be best to keep most of your money in a good bank allowing the broker only enough to properly margin your grain.

31

YOURSELF AND THE MARKET

In your plans for financial success you, yourself, are the most important factor. How you handle yourself will determine just to what extent you can arrive at the full measure of your ambition. When you know the reason for human action you will understand much of the reason for market action. This particular book is directed, for the most part to the 95% who wish to be successful but who have not yet "arrived."

Thomas Hemple Hoyne, the Chicago market writer, says "To keep the upper hand of his own greed and fear is the supreme necessity of him who hopes to win even a chance at success in speculation." The fear of loss is entirely too natural to be easily brushed aside, therefore, the market operator must understand the necessary steps to avoid being shaken by fear. The fear of loss is the worst enemy and this always comes by the route of overtrading, hence much stress must be placed upon this very old market error. As to the matter of greed that is not so bad as it is a form of ambition posing under an ugly name. Psychology teaches us that an intense desire is at the bottom of all financial success. So true is this that it almost becomes the law of success. Wishing anxiously, and intensely for success in the market is not different from desiring success in any other line of endeavor.

Nothing can be gained by smothering the wish to succeed. Let it be called greed, if it suits anyone to do so but it is the author's opinion that the more determined one is, the more anxious he becomes to acquire wealth or success, the more he will study and persevere in his effort to achieve his desired form of success.

If one is upset by fear of loss there is something wrong with his method. He is not going about his work right. He will act rashly and lose. It is futile to attempt to crush the established habits of the race. The proper thing to do is to revise trading habits so they will fit into the powerful human habits and thus add to one's personal ability to succeed.

When reduced to the last analysis the number of reasons for failure in market operations are very few. Complex as the market seems the reader may be surprised to know that there are not more than a half dozen important habits or laws of market action. Exactly the same thing is true of traders' habits. The bad habits are few but they are very bad.

Did you ever go into an exchange when the crowd was bullish and the market advancing to suit their taste? Listen to the jubilant voices, the geniality, the witticisms, the pleasure and feeling in the greetings of men. Things are going their way. They are happy and at their best. They think clearly, their judgment is good. They are pleased because success seems near and success is a powerful stimulant. The reason for this happy feeling is because those men are operating in harmony with market laws. One of the reasons for the great popularity of the bull market is because the mass of traders is working in harmony with human habits and market habits. Therefore, it is of extreme importance that the trader learn early in his market career the close analogy between his own habits and those of the market in which he is operating. The wheat trader who owns a controlling interest in his emotions is more fortunate than the man who owns a controlling interest in an oil well. Sensible, intelligent market habits are equivalent to gold before coinage.

> Habit is the finest kind of organized action. It is something you repeat so often that your subconscious mind takes it up and does the work for you.

A bad habit is to ask others what they think of the market. It is the most common and foolish habit known to traders. The person of whom you ask this question has probably not given the market a fraction of the study which you have. How, therefore, can his opinion be of value to you? Let people chatter about the market as much as they please but keep your own counsel and use your own head. All big results, all notable achievements of construction such as the building of a dam, of a skyscraper, of a rail- or of a big business are through the initiative of one man. "All great institutions," said Emerson, "are the lengthened shadow of a man."

DEVELOP YOUR FORECASTING ABILITY

You have a taste for the market. If not you would not be in possession of this book. You are interested in conquering the market and for that reason have paid out your money to learn, as far as you can from these pages, new and better means of using the market. Having acquired a taste for market operations it will stay with you through life. There will never be a time when you will not thrill to the rapid vibrations of an active market. You will want to be in these movements and will likely get into them. Therefore, it is a matter of simple judgment that you should prepare yourself to the extent of your time and ability to understand and use the market correctly. Only in that direction lies success. The demand is so intense for any kind of a method that will assist in the use of the market that men are using all of their power to acquire a clear working knowledge of market action. The profits from correct trading are large and the dangers of faulty trading are serious, therefore, the intelligent and ambitious market operator will discover the fact that he must learn to trade successfully or be in danger of financial annihilation.

In every exchange will be seen men from middle to old age who have lost their all and who yet hang around the quotation board watching with wistful eyes the quotations which in other days became their undoing. They followed the easy route of substituting guesswork for knowledge and are paying the penalty.

The point the author wishes to impress upon his readers is that simple intelligence tells every trader that he must decide once and for all to master the market or yield ungracefully and let it master him. The market is a great institution. It is the finished product of years of marketing. For some strange reason it exerts a very definite spell over the person who uses it and the only outlet, the only way to success is to learn to master it. When you do that you accomplish two things, you acquire the valuable habit of self-control and put yourself in possession of knowledge that will add to your financial reserves as long as you live.

MAKE BIG PLANS

The chief aim of life is business success and one may as well aim high. Hold your job or work at your profession but go beyond these and add more to your income. The sheer act of saving, valuable as the habit is, will not make anyone wealthy in time to enjoy it. Wages are necessary but they will do little more than make a living. You may live an industrious, toilsome life, earning your wages year in and year out, paying your taxes, your lodge dues, your gas bills and your preacher and in the end have enough left to pay the undertaker but you will never feel the thrill and the power that comes with the making of abundant profits. "Nothing venture, nothing have," says the old proverb. One can pinch out the joy of life by scraping and saving and fearing to risk a few dollars in a speculative enterprise. Vast fortunes have been created by starting speculation in a few shares of stocks as a sideline and by reinvesting the profits until they grew into sizable fortunes.

"Make no little plans," says Robert Burnham in a plea for action. "They have no magic in them to stir men's blood. Make big plans. Aim high and hope and work. Big men dream big things and bring them to pass."

No ambitious man can afford to jeopardize his future by foolishly and carelessly yielding up sums of his accumulated funds in the old fruitless way of trading.

"The burned child fears the fire" and keeps away from it but the scorched trader goes back to trade in the same old way and is scorched again.

But better information is now available. The market is being studied, analyzed and put into harness. For six thousand years the human race watched the flashes of lightning cut through the heavens and knew that some great power lay behind each zig-zag flash of light but only within the last fifty years have the laws of electricity been discovered. Development in any science comes slowly, but it comes.

STATISTICAL INFORMATION.

Much crop information is available but most of it is unimportant. Government crop reports are issued about the tenth of each month giving crop conditions, acreage and estimated yields. The government report is the most reliable of any reports issued although several of the Chicago grain houses have field men out constantly observing the crops who make reports similar to the government reports and often nearly as accurate.

Trading cannot be made successful by following crop reports even though they be distinctly bullish or distinctly bearish. The reason is because traders in all parts of the country are observing the crops and when they make a trade in the market they register their opinion of the crop. Hence the market often discounts a bearish or a bullish report days before the report arrives. It is therefore useless to attempt to follow the grain market on these monthly reports. Other statistical matter is being constantly placed before the trader in the market pages of newspapers and in wire bulletins which reach the exchanges but the safe course is to pay little attention to these, devoting one's energies to following the charted action of the market as the surest means of acquiring success.

As a matter of personal knowledge and market information it is well to keep informed on crop conditions to use in comparison with past years. A grain market review is published in Kansas City and another one in Chicago. These are most excellent records not only of crop reports and other statistics but they give the daily open, high, low and close of all grains and of the principal foreign markets. They should be filed daily and kept for future use. Weather is the great crop magician. Watch that carefully. Nearly all bull markets originate from crop damage and even at the time you are reading this, weather events in some part of north America or elsewhere may be laying the foundation for the next big move.

INEFFECTIVENESS OF FARM AID

A favorite policy of governments is that of attempting to stabilize prices for the benefit of agriculture. These attempts never prove successful yet nations never seem to learn the real reason why they fail. In 1929 our government established the Marketing Act and the farm board in the most pretentious stabilizing plan ever devised. Although we had the failure of the English rubber syndicate, the Brazilian coffee scheme and the Canadian wheat pool all before us as examples of why stabilization would not work, yet our government was not satisfied until it, too, went down to defeat in attempting to stabilize wheat. Overproduction and underproduction are the direct result of prices with weather helping as a secondary factor. All through history, high prices caused by war have resulted in overproduction and lower prices. There is no escape from this cycle and all the money which can be poured into the market to stop a declining price is futile and will be lost.

The U. S. farm board with $500,000,000 at its command began "stabilizing" wheat in 1929 around $1.21 for Chicago wheat. By 1932 the price of wheat with scarcely an appreciable rally had dropped down to 45c, and the board, after having held at one time 329,000,000 bushels, was struggling desperately to sell out a few remaining bushels at the low prices of July, 1932. Thus our stabilizing scheme began at a high point in the market and was sold out at the low of the market. This is recognized as the worst possible market policy and no matter whether men are bound together in a board or are working separately it is impossible to thwart a market which is being corrected by economic conditions. Whenever speculators who are often our business men are free to trade in wheat without restrictions or limitations the market is active, prices are well sustained and the crops of the country are easily marketed. Whenever laws of restriction are enacted against them the market wilts, prices decline and irreparable ruin happens to agriculture.

SPECULATION THE SOUL OF PROGRESS

Lawmakers become so centered in establishing restrictions for various public activities that they often completely lose sight of the background of those things which have brought about our present state of civilization. It has happened during the last hundred years while the New York Stock Exchange was developing a means for marketing securities and the Board of Trade at Chicago was developing a grain market, that public participation has been made easy in these markets. With this ease of operation the attention of the nation in estimating its prosperity has been centered largely in these two liquid markets. The public has come to judge the intensity of our business activity by the way these markets act and in fact a large percentage of the population indulges in these markets for the purpose of securing profits, or of enhancing their business. The miller hedges his grain in the grain market, the banker invests his surplus money in the stock market. Thus the country's state of prosperity is largely registered by the day to day activities of the two markets.

With these keen activities it is natural that abuses sprang up as they do in every branch of human endeavor. Unfortunately Congress with little knowledge of economics but with an intense desire to enact a law against something, has singled out the stock market and the grain market for specific restrictions and has gone to the extent of crippling the markets to where they no longer represent the actual value of wheat and corn, or of securities. Congress has failed to see through and protect our greatest factor of progress, that of speculation. Every big enterprise, every transcontinental railway, every form of development in our business life is the direct result of the speculative urge in men. They believe in the future, they risk their judgment on the future, they see through the present to the big results in the distant beyond, every step of which is directly the result of the natural speculative urge in mankind.

PERSISTENCE

"Nothing in the world can take the place of persistence. Talent will not; nothing is more common than unsuccessful men with talent. Genius will not; unrewarded genius is almost a proverb. Education will not; the world is full of educated derelicts. Persistence and determination alone are omnipotent. The slogan 'Press on' has solved and always will solve the problem of the human race."

—Calvin Coolidge.

BOOK TWO

"The man who plans great things, who studies and works for great things and who expects great things is apt to achieve great things."

The three architects who designed the Taj Mahal, the famous marble building of India, set out to make the most beautiful building in the world and did it. Eiffel, the Frenchman, wishing to erect the world's tallest structure built a steel tower that for forty years held the altitude record and brought the designer undying fame. Harriman and Hill dreamed of transcontinental railroads and built them. Rockefeller, by visioning the great benefits of oil to the world, laid the foundation for the greatest corporation in history. Henry Ford, with prophetic vision, saw the need of a low priced car to suit the masses and was able to establish the greatest single factory ever known. Lindbergh planned a direct "solo" flight from New York to Paris. "Let's go," he said one bright morning and thirty-three hours later landed on the Paris flying field. Great feats, great structures, great fortunes are the direct results of men planning to do great things.

THE USE OF MARKET "KEYS"

Market keys are means of detecting turns in the market. They are
indispensable to the trader. The use of keys has been criticized by
some for the reason that a large number of useless, ineffective keys
have been given out that confuse rather than assist the trader.
Any indication which will assist the trader in discovering a turn
is highly appreciated but this very need often leads traders to accept keys which are of no value.

The daily making and using of charts for forecasting purposes in
the author's office has very naturally disclosed certain types of top
and bottom action that are clear and decisive. They are of great
value and fortunately are few in number.

The detecting of market turns cannot be accomplished by judgment
or a mere act of thought. "Hunches" are worthless and misleading.
The most learned analyst of the market will usually fail to give the
trader anything more than a general view. Market keys must be
used at times in order to operate successfully and these keys are
derived solely from market action. Not all big movements in the
market are forecasted by keys but other methods will be found in
these books which take the place of keys and are fully as efficient.
Prices are strictly a product of thought. All movements have a
reason although often the reason is hidden. It takes time for the
market to disclose its intentions and these keys are used to show
the first definite signs that the market is making a turn. Not
every upswing shows a distinct top day action although most of
them do. Neither does every downswing show a distinct bottom
day. A key may show that the market is undergoing bottom action
but not show the day on which it makes the exact bottom. It is not
so important that the top day be confirmed but that the top be confirmed and the same argument holds true for the bottom.

THE CAUSE OF TURNS

Market orders are pouring in to the exchanges from every corner of the land during the market session. Sometimes it will happen that the majority of these wire orders arriving are bullish and in that case, the market will turn upward. Occasionally it happens that after a considerable advance there comes a day when the volume of trading is sharply bearish, that is, most of the orders are sales. In that case the market turns downward. Throughout this course will be found various methods of detecting not only the turns but the expected extent of movements but this particular book deals specifically with three keys with which the trader should acquaint himself early in his studies.

MARKET KEYS ENDURE

They have their origin, not in variable statistics or in changing weather but in the habits of human beings. They have existed ever since markets were established and operate the same today as they did fifty years ago. By careful charting of daily movements along with close observation of the action it is possible to disclose these valuable indications and bring them out into the clear light where the student trader can use them. Key movements are few because the basic movements of the market are few and they are not confusing when once the trader understands their meaning. The three keys which the author wishes to present to his readers in this book are as follows:

Key Number One—SIGNS OF A STRONG MOVE.

Key Number Two—THE TOP SIGNAL.

Key Number Three—DETECTING THE TREND.

A FORMER BOOKLET

Several years'ago the author published a small book entitled "TEN FAMOUS MASTER KEYS" which sold widely throughout the country. The keys were all very useful but more recent study has enabled the author to eliminate most of these keys and to reconstruct the three best ones into a form that makes them far better than when spread out in ten different keys. In describing the use of these keys charts of recent market action have been used, most of which are within the memory of the reader.

Key Number One—SIGNS OF A STRONG MOVE.

The type of action most desired and most patiently waited for is the beginning of a genuinely substantial advance. One that will not fade out after a few days sharp movement but will continue upward for weeks or months to a high top. The student will be surprised to know that strong, decisive and measurable advances take place almost every year. During the last ten years there have been eleven bull markets. These big movements quickly fade out of the public memory and find the people always unprepared for the next one. The object of this key is to show the studious trader when the market is coming out of a bottom congestion and is heading for a big advance. The style of movement which we term "big advance" refers almost entirely to bull movements. Later in this course the reader will get explicit instructions about how to forecast and use these bull movements but KEY NUMBER ONE is placed before the reader now as one of the earlier steps in detecting big movements which he will better understand before he finishes the course. Four stages appear in key number one.

Final liquidation	Double bottom
Accumulation	Signs of advance

One or two of these stages may be absent without destroying the effectiveness of the key.

5

CHART OF SEPTEMBER WHEAT, 1927

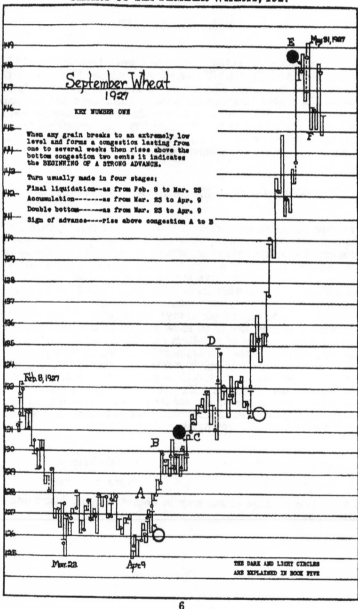

September Wheat
1927

KEY NUMBER ONE

When any grain breaks to an extremely low
level and forms a congestion lasting from
one to several weeks then rises above the
bottom congestion two cents it indicates
the BEGINNING OF A STRONG ADVANCE.

Turn usually made in four stages:

Final liquidation--as from Feb. 8 to Mar. 23

Accumulation--------as from Mar. 23 to Apr. 9

Double bottom-------as from Mar. 23 to Apr. 9

Sign of advance----rise above congestion A to B

Feb. 8, 1927

May 31, 1927

Mar. 23   Apr. 9

THE DARK AND LIGHT CIRCLES
ARE EXPLAINED IN BOOK FIVE

KEY NUMBER ONE

When any grain breaks to an extremely low level and forms a narrow bottom congestion lasting from one to several weeks, then advances two cents above the congestion, it indicates the BEGINNING OF A STRONG ADVANCE.

A very common habit of the grain options is to drag slowly along sidewise not far above the bottom levels of the last bear market, then undergo a sharp drop of a few cents which is termed "final liquidation." Note this in the chart on page 6 where a break of eight cents from Feb. 8 to March 23 finished the decline by completing liquidation in the option.

From March 23 to April 9 is a period of congestion called "accumulation" but which is more properly a period of uncertainty when traders are endeavoring to determine whether the price should be higher or lower. Professional traders usually accumulate part of their lines of long wheat on such occasions.

From April 9 an advance begins which rises above the top of the bottom congestion at A. This is the first sign that an extensive movement upward is forming. By the time the advance reaches B, two cents above the bottom congestion, enough public interest is created to invite further buying and the advance continues. Such sharp advances grow in intensity all the way up until the top is reached.

During the congestion period from March 23 to April 9 a small "double bottom" effect is noted. This often happens but is not important.

The definite sign of the advance is when the price moves above the congestion as from A to B. That is the logical time to buy as it is definitely established that the market is on the way up and that declines thereafter will be only small reactions. This is one of the best keys known and may be used at the start of many bull movements.

7

Not every big advance starts from a bottom congestion. Occasionally though not frequently an advance will start from the dissemination of unexpected news. For instance in June 1929, when the wheat price had dropped rapidly down to 96, an announcement appeared in large heading in a Chicago paper that the farm board had just received its first 100 million dollars with which to stop the break in wheat. Immediately, and without making any bottom congestion at all the price rushed up ten cents and eventually rose sixty cents having been started by a news announcement that was false.

(The facts are that the board was being appointed but at the time did not have a dollar in its possession. The newspaper made a huge mistake but the fact that it sent prices up "exonerated" the paper and pleased the members of the newly appointed board at the prospects of the power possible for the board to use).

The usual cause of the "liquidation break" is that large traders will not enter the market until they can buy up their initial lots at a very low price. It is well known that smaller traders, after so long a time, will sell out their long grain and it is this event that causes the final liquidation break and which offers such an excellent opportunity for the skillful trader. It is said some times that these gentlemen "assist the break" by selling the market down to force out the remaining longs. This cannot be confirmed but is probably true.

Later in this course the reader will discover that such breaks as that from February 8 to March 23 may be utilized by any trader as they have a very definite meaning. It is not only a liquidation break but is also a "vertical break," a very important phenomena in market action which is fully described in Book Number Four.
The light and dark circles shown on the chart are very important but cannot be taken up at this time. They are fully discussed and explained in Book Number Five. It has been the aim of the author to make the course one of increasing interest from the first book to the last page of the last one.

APPLYING KEY NUMBER ONE TO CORN

The key movements in corn are similar to those in wheat although there are certain differences in the general market action of the two grains. On the following page you will find a chart of December corn for the year 1930. This comprised a bull movement in corn at a time when there was no bull movement in wheat. It is therefore an independent corn movement and is one of the best seen in the corn market for years. The movement was caused by hot, dry weather in July and early August.

In this corn chart you will note the top just before final liquidation was at 78 from which point the market broke rapidly to around 68. In this case there was no double bottom such as noted in the wheat chart but simply a period of congestion lasting nearly one month from June 16 to July 12. We thus have the final break and the bottom congestion up to July 12, then begins a movement that carries the price up through A to B or two cents above the bottom congestion. This is the sign of a strong advance and as you will note the movement was completed by August 7 about three weeks later.

Thus KEY NUMBER ONE as applied to this corn movement shows:

FIRST— Final liquidation from 78 down to the 66 level.

SECOND—Accumulation between 66 and 71.

THIRD— Breaks out of congestion from A to B.

There was no double bottom in this congestion which, however, is an unimportant matter. Now the application of this to practical use is very clear. If the reader had before him the charted action of this grain up to July 12, he would be aware of the fact that the market was preparing for a sharp movement as all markets eventually move out of a "rut" with a strong one-way movement. When the price got up to B he would know that a big move was beginning and if he had not already bought grain during the congestion period he would buy when the price got up to the 73 level as shown at B.

9

KEY NO. 1 — CORN CHART

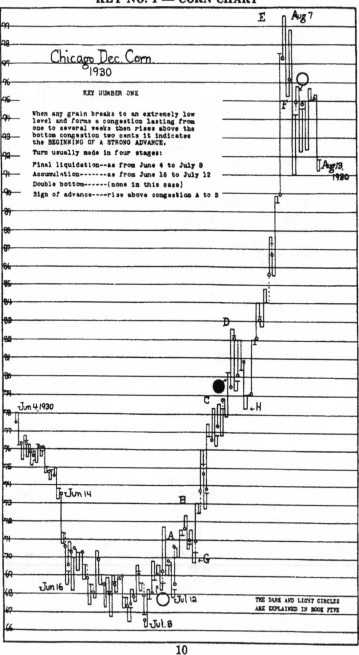

Chicago Dec. Corn.
1930

KEY NUMBER ONE

When any grain breaks to an extremely low
level and forms a congestion lasting from
one to several weeks then rises above the
bottom congestion two cents it indicates
the BEGINNING OF A STRONG ADVANCE.

Turn usually made in four stages:

Final liquidation--as from June 4 to July 9
Accumulation--------as from June 16 to July 12
Double bottom------(none in this case)
Sign of advance----rise above congestion A to B

THE DARK AND LIGHT CIRCLES
ARE EXPLAINED IN BOOK FIVE

10

APPLYING KEY NUMBER ONE TO RYE

While rye is the most erratic of all the grains in its market action yet it conforms generally to the habits of the wheat options. The volume of trading in rye is less than one-tenth of the trading in wheat.

In this rye example the stage of final liquidation was too far back to show it upon the chart but it was there. One of the advantages derived from this key is that it shows the trend early in the move. Large operators, in following a strong advance, often buy large amounts of wheat on a reaction of two or three cents, then sell out part of the grain on the next rally. Those who like this form of trading will find this key highly valuable as it establishes the trend for them. Trading can be done on one side until the trend is complete.

The general belief that skilled or professional operators get in at the bottom and out at the top is only partially correct. Initial deals, made by these gentlemen, are usually quite correct but before a movement is through they are apt to become confused. A very clear chart showing how big operators hit the market and how they miss it sadly at times is shown in Book Number Four.

The only convenient way to fully understand how a grain is preparing for a big movement and to be able to detect this movement by the use of a key is to keep an accurate daily chart of the option in which you are interested. The time to watch for the appearance of KEY NUMBER ONE is after a long persistent break when prices look hopeless. The final break of a bear market is the final liquidation that takes place in KEY NUMBER ONE. Whenever an option of grain breaks to a low point and begins to work in a narrow range the trader should be on the lookout for the signs of a strong advance which will most certainly come when the price gets above the bottom congestion.

11

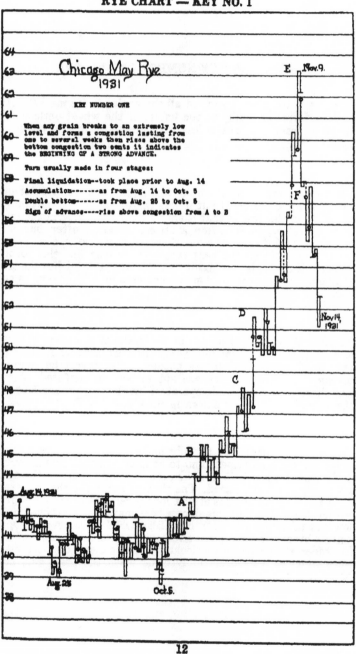

Chicago May Rye
1931

KEY NUMBER ONE

When any grain breaks to an extremely low
level and forms a congestion lasting from
one to several weeks then rises above the
bottom congestion two cents it indicates
the BEGINNING OF A STRONG ADVANCE.

Turn usually made in four stages:

Final liquidation--took place prior to Aug. 14

Accumulation--------as from Aug. 14 to Oct. 5

Double bottom------as from Aug. 25 to Oct. 5

Sign of advance----rise above congestion from A to B

KEY NUMBER TWO

The Top Signal

When a grain option advances rapidly closing sharply higher each day for two or more days, then abruptly closes a cent or two lower, it is a signal that top is made or is near.

This key is extremely useful because it comes into the market when it is necessary to conserve profits. Like KEY NUMBER ONE it is not a key for frequent use as it occurs only when there has been a completed bull market or a big swing almost as extensive as a bull market.

After KEY NUMBER ONE has shown the student trader how to buy into a movement, his next concern will be how to get out with the largest profit or in other words how to correctly estimate the top. That is the object of KEY NUMBER TWO and it is an admirable one for the purpose. Other methods of estimating tops will be given later on so that, by the use of KEY NUMBER TWO and the other information acquired in this course later, the trader can almost certainly pick the top of his market and sell out his long grain.

The outstanding achievement of any grain trader is to buy as near the bottom as possible and to sell out as near the top as possible. It is not only a profitable feat but it will engage all of the ingenuity and intelligence of the trader to accomplish the feat. This key will be found extremely useful.

No rule or key in the market may be expected to work perfectly all the time. The chances are that this key, also KEY NUMBER ONE will seldom fail you. Later on you will be shown how the keys may be combined with certain market laws and thus get the combined force of two or three powerful indications or market factors. For the present we will confine our attention to the simple, initial use of the key, remembering that KEY NUMBER ONE is for the bottom and KEY NUMBER TWO for the top.

In explaining the use of KEY NUMBER TWO seven different tops are shown in the accompanying charts. There is naturally some variance in this top action but it is clearly discernible that this key points out the top action in each movement. With the student trader the question will arise as to what causes a top in the market. A movement makes top when the volume of selling exceeds the volume of buying. It starts from the profit taking of professional and other heavy traders who believe the movement has gone as far as it can hold up. Many of these men use private "indications" and rules similar to what the reader sees in this book and are able to estimate the top with far greater accuracy than the average trader. This initial profit taking drives the market downward and brings in a host of short sellers who have been waiting for the break that always follows a high top. Professionals join the shorts and put out a "line" of short sales thus accelerating the decline.

In the use of KEY NUMBER TWO the trader should be on the look-out for signs of a "double top." This occurs in many bull markets but not in all of them. The cause at the root of the double top movement is that too many traders sell the market short after a top has been made so that an oversold condition develops in the early stages of the decline. Shrewd traders become aware of this over-sold condition and buy for a rally, knowing that the short traders will be forced to cover. The double top charts shown later in this book illustrate how the market gathers and undergoes a second advance known as the double top.

Four examples of tops in which KEY NUMBER TWO is used are given on the succeeding two pages. It may be added that every style of movement usable by the trader is pictured in the graphs of this course which cover the last ten years of market action or from 1922 to 1932. The office of KEY NUMBER ONE is to detect a new uptrend at its beginning while that of KEY NUMBER TWO is to detect a new downtrend at its beginning. Nearly all rules and keys are for the very important purpose of determining market trend.

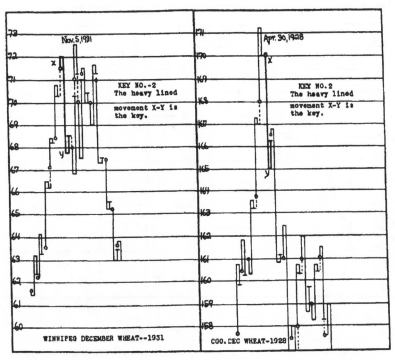

Winnipeg Wheat — 1931   Chicago Dec. Wheat — 1928

KEY NUMBER TWO—When a grain option advances rapidly closing sharply higher each day for two or more days then abruptly closes a cent or two lower it is a signal that top is made or is near.

Advances which make rapid strides and sharp tops as above shown usually start from very low levels. Almost every movement starting with KEY NUMBER ONE will end with a top similar to those above and is therefore forecastable by the use of KEY NUMBER TWO. In this way the trader may start, making his purchases at the bottom and finish by taking profits at approximately top figures.

On the day the market "closes a cent or two lower" it is possible to tell fifteen or twenty minutes before the close that this is to happen, thus affording the trader a chance to sell out before the close of the first down day. Sometimes it happens that the market will develop another day's rally, going higher than the Key Day—as shown in the Winnipeg chart above—but the advance is spent nevertheless and all long wheat should be sold out.

15

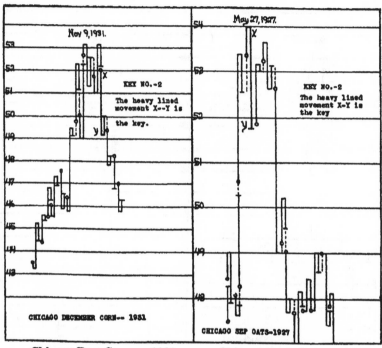

Chicago Dec. Corn — 1931   Chicago Sept. Oats — 1927

KEY NUMBER TWO USED IN CORN AND OATS

When corn has a bull movement independently of wheat, as the corn movement shown on page 10 of this book, the top will be sharp. However the key day is clear as may be noted. When corn is merely moving in sympathy with a bull move in wheat the top will not be very high and will be rather "flat." Such a flat top is shown in the corn chart above, yet the key day X-Y gives the top signal very decisively and may be acted upon with confidence by the trader.

On page 12 is found a graph of Rye with a sharp top made forecastable by using KEY NUMBER TWO. By running through the graphs of the several books in this course many instances will be seen of the action of these two keys. It is not possible to show the keys in each case as it would cumber the graphs with too much descriptive matter.

Brilliant and useful as these keys are the reader will find still other and more remarkable methods for forecasting as he proceeds in this course. Every new thing learned is a further step towards a complete market education.

16

A STUDY OF TRENDS

To know the trend is the most important information the trader can have. Without this knowledge he will make costly mistakes and, in fact, will play a losing game until he gets right with the main trend. First of all the trend is not difficult to understand or to determine. The chief obstacle met by the trader is his own lack of confidence. He wonders if the market will run true to form this time. This constant Doubting Thomas attitude defeats many traders even after they have made a correct and clear analysis of the market. The market student can have no better means of forecasting movements than to compare the market he is charting with the various charts of this course. Somewhere amongst them he will find a movement that practically duplicates the one in which he is interested. Twenty years after this set of books is published the movements of the grains will be following the same keys, rules and laws which the student is now studying.

TREND IS ALWAYS UPWARD OR DOWNWARD

In other words the movements of a market are always in major uptrend or major downtrend because price movements are forever running to extremes—too high or too low.

When the price is too low certain economic and psychological changes take place that cause the public to turn about face and to continue in that direction until the price is too high.

When a bear market has nearly completed bottom it may drag along for months waiting for bullish developments of sufficient force to start the price up again. Such an instance will be found in the bear market (for the great depression) which made bottom in October 1931 and drifted along until the latter half of 1932 before showing signs of uptrend.

After a bull market top the market seldom drifts "sidewise" although there are occasionally such instances. After a bear market has made its approximate bottom the market nearly always drifts for a few weeks or a few months before returning to uptrend.

TREND CAUSED BY CROP CONDITIONS

Nearly all bull movements are caused by short crops and most bear markets by ample crop supplies. Occasionally a war comes along to furnish a bull market but since big wars come only about once in twenty to thirty years the trader had best fall back upon crop conditions as the origin of big movements. The long sustained uptrends have been caused by wars but they are few and far apart.

> The Thirty Years War in Germany 1618-1648.
> The Napoleonic Wars lasting from 1795-1815.
> The Great War, lasting from 1914-1918.

There is a very persistent **economic trend**—either towards overproduction or underproduction—running through the market all the time which causes the enormously high prices such as those which prevailed during the war or those which prevailed during the great depression. These are caused by crop conditions but may be ignored as many bull and bear movements may take place during either economic uptrend or economic downtrend.

During the six and one-half years of economic downtrend from 1925 to 1931 nine bull and nine bear markets occurred.

Great overproduction occurred from 1880 to 1894 with the advent of the newly invented self binder and again in 1925 to 1931 with the introduction of tractors and combines for the harvesting of wheat. Thus the two most serious price declines during the past fifty years have been caused by labor saving wheat machinery.

> Now that overproduction, assisted by the depression, has driven wheat prices down to the lowest point for seventy-five years, production will be forcibly curtailed and a long economic uptrend will prevail. This will be interspersed with many bull and bear markets, all of them working in accord with market law and each movement possible to follow by methods taught in this market course.

KEY NUMBER THREE

Detecting the Trend

TREND IS DOWN FROM THE TOP OF A BULL MOVE-
MENT UNTIL THE PRICE IS APPROXIMATELY
DOWN TO THE LEVEL FROM WHICH THE LAST
BULL MOVEMENT ORIGINATED.
TREND IS UP FROM THE TIME A BEAR MARKET IS
COMPLETED UNTIL THE NEXT BULL MARKET
MAKES TOP.

Trend may, therefore, be determined at any time by simply referring
back to the last big movement of a grain. If the most recent **big
movement** was a bull movement with a high top, then the trend
you are seeking is a major down trend. It may display some sharp
rallies but the trend is irrevocably downward until a complete bear
market is finished.

If the most recent **big movement** has been in the form of a long decline with prices surprisingly low or about where the last bull movement originated, then the trend is upward and while it may work
up slowly for awhile, nothing will stop the advance until the market
has made a high top. Therefore, the student may tell at the moment
he learns the past history of his market—the last big move—
whether the trend is in major uptrend or major downtrend.

**It is evident that charts are indispensable for detecting
past movements. If the student has neither the past market quotations nor charts of past movements he may order
charts from the author. Chart of any grain option complete $2.00.**

On pages 20 and 21 is shown a six months bull movement starting
slowly after a vertical break of ten cents in October 1927. This
was the "final liquidation" break seen in KEY NUMBER ONE.
From that time onward a trader who had the chart before him
would understand that wheat was a purchase on any moderate reaction as the **major trend was upward.**

19

The six months bull wheat movement shown on these two pages is particularly useful in that it shows how the advance was followed up by the author's Daily Grain Service. The first "special wire" was sent when the price rose above the bottom congestion at A-B. After that other wires to "buy wheat" were sent as the market rose above congestions.

Movements which start according to KEY No. 1 as this one did, are headed for a sharp, high top and the trader operating in such a market will know, after reading this book, that the advance will not end until a **fast, finishing rise** has taken place. Therefore, he will hold purchases bought at the various levels and buy more, just as we advised our subscribers, along the way up. Then at the top KEY NUMBER TWO comes into play and all long wheat is sold out.

KEY NUMBER THREE shows the trader that wheat was a purchase at any stage of the movement until fast action developed. Trend was upward because, having started from a very low level (or bear market bottom) the trend would be up until a rapid rise developed even if it took months to develop this fast top action.

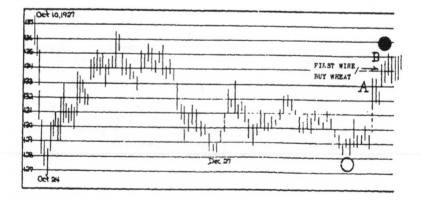

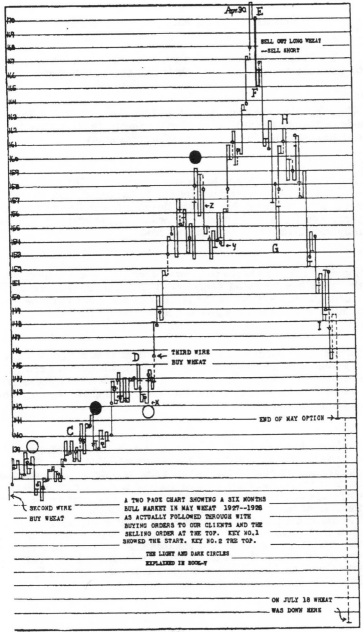

A TWO PAGE CHART SHOWING A SIX MONTHS
BULL MARKET IN MAY WHEAT 1927--1928
AS ACTUALLY FOLLOWED THROUGH WITH
BUYING ORDERS TO OUR CLIENTS AND THE
SELLING ORDER AT THE TOP. KEY NO.1
SHOWED THE START. KEY NO.2 THE TOP.

THE LIGHT AND DARK CIRCLES
EXPLAINED IN BOOK-V

WORKING WITH KEY NUMBER THREE

The key is very useful as it is needed the moment a trader decides to enter the market, and will show him the correct trend.

When the trend has been determined then the trader can follow one side of the market until it reaches its finish. Several ways to detect top are given in this course of market study.

Should the trader chance to become interested in the market after top has been made, he will understand by the use of KEY NUMBER TWO that the trend has turned downward and he can take the short side for a long break. He will, also, understand that any rally during the bear trend will not hold.

Should the trader chance to become interested in the market when the price has advanced considerably and yet no fast top action shown as, for instance, at the point D he will know that the trend is still upward and the move not nearly complete.

On the other hand, should he enter the market somewhere about the point H he will know that the bull market is over and that sales are in order because the trend will be downward until the price eventually approaches its starting place, as is shown on July 18th at the bottom of page 21.

All bear markets do not go down as low as the point from which the rise started but they go approximately to that level. The grain market seldom stays at a normal price very long. It is eternally running the gamut from an extreme low to an extreme high, then down again, therefore the trend is ceaselessly running back and forth from an oversold to an overbought condition and vise versa. The technical position often exerts a greater influence on prices than crop conditions but it takes a comparatively small range of the market to correct a strained technical position. Bull markets are nearly always the result of crop conditions but the public carries them too far. Hence the market becomes technically "overbought."

Technical positions refer chiefly to an overbought or an oversold market.

An overbought market is a stage of the advance where the desire to buy on the part of the trading public overshadows all things else. The market becomes over-bulled, that is people buy heavily at too high prices. They pay so much for the grain that they cannot sell it at a profit and are, therefore, a target for short sellers. The result is a break. How high an overbought market will go can be estimated with reasonable accuracy by means taught later in the course.

An oversold market is the opposite of one that is overbought. Part of an oversold market is the result of speculative trading but an element enters that is not found in an overbought market. It is the hedging of wheat by millers and grain dealers which they buy as it comes into the terminals. This hedging is all in the shape of short sales and adds its weight to a market that is becoming speculatively oversold. No matter how low the price goes hedging sales are put out. Eventually, the price is down so low that the professional trader, discovering a grain being below its real value, begins to buy the grain aggressively as a speculative venture. It is at this juncture that the market discloses the fact that it is oversold. It begins to rise a little higher on each successive rally, causing grain dealers to "lift" their hedges and the tide turns from selling to buying.

An oversold market does not reverse as quickly as the market that is overbought for the reason that the volume of trade and the number of traders is very much smaller at low levels where the market is beginning to be oversold. The price may drag for months waiting for something to start it upward. Usually around the bottom figures, or near bottom, a dragging market causes traders to close out with disgust and thus we get the "final liquidation stage" noted in KEY NUMBER ONE. This brings the market to an acutely oversold condition and nearly always ends the bear market.

23

THE COIL AND STRAIN

A STRAIN in the market position of any option means a tension, an inclination to be drawn back like a rubber band stretched to its limit. Strains work two ways. The market may develop a strain to rally or a strain to break. Sharply bullish news often causes short traders to cover or buy in their wheat and the rally which ensues places the market at a strain. That is the market becomes unbalanced or overbought and, having advanced too rapidly and too high, develops a strong tendency to break back to lower levels again.

Extra bearish news may cause long traders to liquidate their wheat and the break which follows places the market in a strained position in which the tendency is to rally or recover.

A "straight down" break of five to ten cents always develops an intense strain to rally. Sometimes a break goes farther and intensifies the strain. Eventually the market will rise and retrace the ground lost by the break. A "straight up" rally of five to ten cents or more will eventually be followed by a break. This strained position of the market is very important in selecting positions for making a trade. BOOK FOUR goes into STRAINS in more complete detail.

THE COIL is a rut-like or gradually narrowing style of action in a grain option which usually ends with a sharp movement one direction or the other. The author does not consider this type of action particularly important, but places it before the student as a part of his market education. There is little difference between a coil and a congestion. If a sharp break has preceded the coil formation then the market is almost sure to break out of the coil on the upside and for a sharp rally. If a sharp rise occurred previous to the coil formation then the market will break out on the down side and for a considerable break. Coils are narrow and slow at the bottom of bear markets but are wide and rapidly completed when at high figures or after a bull market has made top. On page 25 a graph is shown of a coil about midway between the top and bottom of a bull market.

COIL CHART

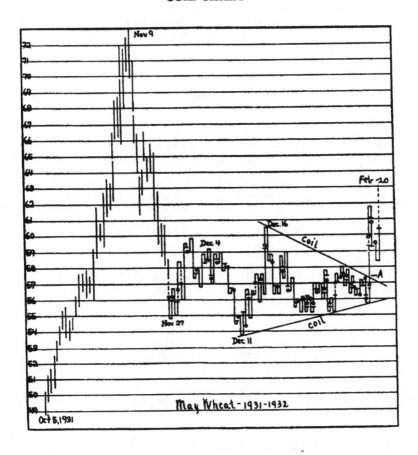

WHAT THE COIL CHART SHOWS

The graph on page 25 was taken from the wheat movements of October to December 1931. The bull movement from October 5 to Nov. 9 was followed by a part way break to the former bottom but around Nov. 27 a coil formation began which finally ended with a moderate rally to 66 or a little higher than shown at Feb. 20.

The reason a coil movement tapers down is because of the lessening volume of trading. Narrowing markets cause traders to leave the market.

As the student gets along farther in this course he will learn from examples of market action that the break from Nov. 9 to Nov. 27 was **not a complete return** to the starting place as usually occurs in bear markets. Therefore, a coil, such as shown in the chart, does **not** indicate any considerable rally even when it breaks out sharply on the upside as at A. The reason is because a further decline even lower than that of December 11 is yet to come to satisfy the bear market law. This is more fully described in BOOK SIX.

The conclusion reached is that the trader should be more influenced by the technical position of the market, the "strains" described on a previous page, than by the coil.

When a period of dullness occurs in market action, no matter from what cause or at what position, the trading clientele becomes intensely concerned as to "which way the price will jump." Chart students and statistical concerns elaborate on these formations and the student trader will hear many fine spun theories as to why the price should move up or down from the "rut."

After years of observation the author places great importance upon the congestion but not much importance on the coil formation. One of the tricks a coil will play is to break through the coil angles on the down side then in a day or two reverse and cut back upward through the coil and out on the upside. The student who charts coils will prove this to his satisfaction.

26

INFLUENCE OF STOCKS ON WHEAT

Since wheat is the leader in the Commodity Market and U. S. Steel the leader in the Securties Market there is naturally a certain bond of sympathy between the two leaders that amounts to sympathy between the two markets.

One market cannot prosper without imparting some of its prosperity to the other. Neither can one suffer heavy liquidation without embarrassing the other. A bull markt in grains naturally adds to the buying power of the farms and brings welcome business to numberless stocks whose products are sold to the country buyers.

But for the trader to try to follow one market by the indications given in the other is to court disaster. A bull movement may have to run its course before stocks "wake up." Also a movement in New York stocks may be on the upgrade for months before just the right crop condition develops to give wheat a send-off.

During these periods when the stock market and grain markets both make bottom at approximately the same time, then the ensuing advance will appear to be a team affair with stocks helping grain and grain helping stocks. But the obsession of traders is that each small movement or day's action in grain is minutely affected by the movement of stocks. This is misleading and untrue. The wheat options can be followed best by watching for the strains, for the key movements and for the high tops or low bottoms of which there will be an ample number all along the way.

As to whether stocks or grains suit the trader best is a question to be settled by each man for himself. A considerable number of stocks show greater activity than wheat at times but weather events affect wheat causing many rapid oscillations in price which may be used by the trader for profits. Wheat may have a bull market every year while it is seldom a stock enjoys such a move more than once in two to four years. Rules and methods used in grains are not all applicable to stock market operations.

A SWING HABIT

A habit of swings so common as to be almost a law of the market is as follows:

> When a grain option moves into new high ground above the top of the previous swing it will eventually drop back to a point even with the top of the previous swing.

This type of movement appears during a period when large swings are frequent, especially after a bull movement has finished and the market is working back downward again. Several charts later on will show the workings of this rule, but it is hardly of enough importance to devote much space to it here. In stocks the same rule holds and occurs more frequently than in grains.

A very excellent example of this was found in Auburn Automobile stock early in 1932. The bottom of a swing in February was around 80. In the spring a break occurred to 28¾ or more than 50 points below the February bottom. Now this swing rule works for breaks as well as for advances, and the natural thing for Auburn was to rally to the 80 level or up to the February bottom. The rally occurred in June, 1932, and 77 was reached or within 3 points of the February bottom. For grains we may therefore quote the following rule for downswings:

> When a grain option breaks into new low ground below the previous downswing it will eventually rally back up to the bottom of the previous downswing.

This rule is of little value in a bull movement, especially the short, quick bull movements, as reactions are small and usually not more than two or three days' duration. In bear markets the rule is highly useful and should be applied as soon as the market begins to make its downward swings. This rule is not indispensable, but adds to the trader's stock of market information.

THE PHILOSOPHY OF PROFITS

One of the marvels of business life is that some men possess what is termed the "money sense" while others appear to be devoid of this faculty. In the business of merchandising men with the money sense become captains of industry. In the market men with this ability become "wizards" or "professionals." In some way they do things differently from the way others do them. They do things the right way rather than the easy way. Those glimpses which the writer has occasionally had of the operations of skilled traders show these men to be particularly skilled in personal self-control. They are not easily disturbed by small market movements or by small talk which may be overheard by them. They avoid overtrading as they would a rattlesnake. They can make a trade according to rules which they follow and then stick to their trades until either the movement occurs or is thwarted. When the time comes to sell they sell all they intend to unload in a hurry. When accumulating a line of wheat these men use the utmost secrecy and spread out their buying over some space of time in order not to put the price up while taking on their lines. Furthermore, they keep ample reserves with which to margin their trades.

THE PHILOSOPHY OF LOSS

This is far simpler and is based upon the weakness of human nature. Summed up into a simple statement:

> The reason people lose in the market is because there is no one to force them to take profits, but there is someone to make them take losses.

When one overtrades and margins get low the broker is forced to close out trades to prevent loss to himself. The broker is non-committal as long as the trader has substantial margins, or a profit, but he will force his client to take a loss rather than take one himself.

29

USE OF THE STOP LOSS

The stop loss order is a very valuable protection at times and at other times it merely serves to take the trader out of a perfectly good trade and leave him out of the market when the move he was playing for comes about. The proper time to use a stop loss is when the trader is in doubt as to the trend or when he is overtrading. Keep these two suggestions in mind. For instance, if the trader was reasonably sure a big move was pending he might be tempted to buy wheat on a four or five cent margin in order to get into the move "on the ground floor." In such case it will be wise to use a two cent stop loss as protection until the expected move is actually well on the way. Then the stop should be moved up a little at a time until there would be little or no loss in case of an unexpected reversal.

In pyramiding on the way up it is wise to keep a stop under the highest trade. If the trader is in well and his first lots stand at a good profit, say ten or twelve cents, then new trades should be protected with a two or three cent stop. Be careful not to trade too heavily on the advance. Keep lots about the same size.

If the trader has carefully analyzed his market and is sure of the trend he need not use a stop on single trades. For instance, when KEY NUMBER TWO shows the top has been made there is no virtue in placing a stop against a short sale. Manifestly the market is in down trend and a close stop might serve only to take him out when a good profit is in prospect.

The use of a stop on all trades is an acknowledgment of faulty reasoning. The trader attempts thus to protect himself against mistakes rather than take the time to study his market. Such use of the stop is certain of ultimate and complete loss. If the student now reading these studies, will use the three keys given at the first of this book, will first decide upon the trend, then follow up with the other two keys, NUMBER ONE and NUMBER TWO, he will be able to trade with very few stops.

DOUBLE TOPS

This course would not be complete without some discussion of the "double top" so often seen in grain movements. Bull movements of wheat and corn often end with a double top, though many such movements end with a sharp top and with hardly any semblance of a double top. This sharp top style of action is seen in the charts on pages 11 and 18. The more lengthy bull movements are inclined to develop double top action, an excellent example being given on page 32.

The double top is caused by heavy buying on the part of disappointed speculators who failed to get in on the rise and are anxious to buy on the first break or by speculators who sold out too early and wish to be in the move again. They miscalculate the outlook, believing the move not nearly over. When the big bull market of 1925 was making top (shown on page 32) the author took particular pains to canvass the brokerage houses to determine the drift of local opinion. Traders, almost to a man, expected wheat to continue up much higher; some expressed $2.50 as the expected top for the move.

This overbullish condition of the public mind kept people buying right up to the last day and when the break had settled back to 177-178 the volume of buying was so heavy that the price rushed back up again to the second top March 2.

The second top is well utilized by professionals in unloading any belated holdings which they failed to sell out on the first top. Professionals also sell short heavily on second tops. By carefully charting the grain in which you are trading it is possible to detect this double top action and profit greatly thereby. Note the following summary:

A double top occurs in about half of the bull moves.

A big swing may have a double top.

Close long grain when KEY NUMBER TWO gives top signal.

The second top may slightly exceed the first top.

DOUBLE BOTTOMS are of less importance than double tops, since they are usually made at the bottom of low markets when the daily action is slow and the daily range narrow. In KEYS NUMBER ONE and NUMBER TWO will be seen small double bottom action.

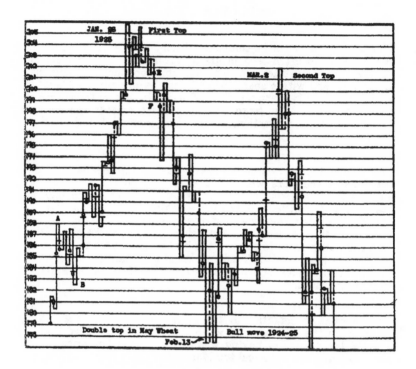

DOUBLE TOP IN WHEAT

A very large double top was made at the conclusion of the big bull wheat movement of 1924-1925. The first top was reached January 28, 1925. The second top March 2, 1925. President Coolidge was up for election for his second term and a short crop promised in Canada served as the fuse to set the movement off. The active start took place in June, following the Canadian Government report. Like all big movements this one went far above the expectations of the trading public. Professional traders estimated the top at 185, which was 20 cents too low. After a bull market makes top it is sold too heavily by traders who use narrow margins. This causes an "oversold" condition when the price is not far down from the top. Professional traders and men who understand market action buy wheat on such breaks and cause a rise which makes the second top as shown at Mar-2. Second tops are particularly good for short selling, as it is the last time up.

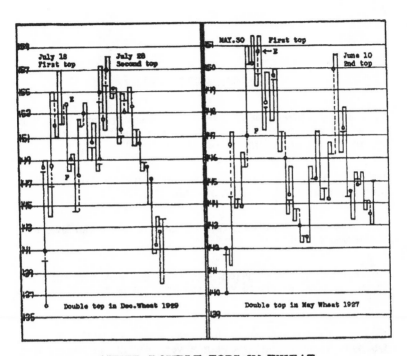

Double top in Dec. Wheat 1929

Double top in May Wheat 1927

OTHER DOUBLE TOPS IN WHEAT

DECEMBER WHEAT in 1929, as above shown, made a very excellent double top in which the second top was slightly higher than the first. Again the top key (Number Two) shows the place to get out of longs. Note the heavy lined day E-F in each chart. When this signal appears the trader should not wait for a possible second top, as too many of the bull moves fade out without the formality of a second time up. The larger the bull movement the more likely the second top.

The first break of over twelve cents from the top made July 18 is conclusive evidence to the trader that any further rally will be a second top and is to be used as a place to sell short. He need not be disturbed because an over-bullish state of mind amongst traders causes a slightly higher price on the second time up. "Professionals" well understand this type of action and sell short heavily—especially on the second top.

MAY WHEAT in 1927, as above shown, made a very clear double top, gave the top signal at E-F and became an excellent short sale at the time the E-F signal was shown. These top actions are always very sharp and stops should be carried down to protect short sale profits until the trader is taken out on his stop.

RESISTANCE LEVELS

This phrase is often met with in market literature, and while it is not of great importance it is well that the student be apprized of its relative importance in market usage.

Whenever the price of an option rallies repeatedly from a certain level it is considered a "resistance point."

Whenever an option breaks several times from a given level it is considered a "resistance level."

By referring to the chart on page 6 of this book you will see a resistance point developed when the price touched 125 the second time and rallied therefrom.

On page 12 is a rye chart which shows a resistance level at 39 to 40. On page 25 is a chart showing a very definite resistance level where wheat touched 55⅛ five times during a period of eleven days. The cause of this was that certain traders gave orders to their brokers to buy all wheat offered at 55⅛.

Winnipeg October wheat, during the summer of 1932 dropped to around 56, where it remained in a narrow zone of action for seven weeks. Therefore, 56 was the resistance level. Also it became a bottom congestion. When the price rose above that congestion a sharp advance developed.

Resistance levels occur at the tops of rallies at times, as will be noted in the various charts in these books. Top levels are not long protracted, as the market is active when high, and it is seldom the price tarries more than three to four days before breaking lower.

Top resistance levels are sometimes designated as "pressure," which means some heavy trader or group of traders is selling out long wheat or selling short at a given level. The effect is that the advance stopped each time it reached the selling level.

THE 50% REACTION

This common type of action is not dependable, though it will be found as a favorite topic amongst in and out traders. The theory is that a rally will extend half as far as the last break. Also that a break will extend at least half as far down as the last rally. This applies to daily movements or to swings. Later in this course the student will discover a much better way to use the swings by what is termed "vertical breaks" and "vertical advances." The 50% reaction is so undependable that the author can suggest no rule which will help the trader.

SCALPING

This is the common name for in and out trading where the trader expects to take only a small profit or "scalp" from the market. It more often results in taking the trader's scalp. Only those who haunt the brokerage houses attempt scalping. Merchants or others who stay away from the exchange make their trades with a definite long pull idea in view and are more often successful than in and out traders. The man who stays close to the exchange under the belief that he has to have a constant stream of information must also meet a steady stream of variable comment. Bulletins bring in a constant crossfire of opinions and to these is added the mixture of street opinions with the result that a man must have an iron bound will and unwavering intelligence to trade successfully by the in and out or scalping method.

It has long been a fond hope that a method might be found that would enable the trader to "sit astride the daily actions" and ride them to an unerring profit. This is no nearer realization than it was forty years ago. Buying or selling wheat when at preferred positions, as the student is shown in this book, will excel any scheme or artifice used for daily action trading. By the use of KEY NUMBER ONE more money can be made in a single big movement than can be made in a long campaign of in and out trading. It is the "one way market" that makes the money.

Quick profits are the eternal lure of the speculator, but they are like the fabled "lorelei" of the Rhineland whose dulcet music led the enchanted traveler to a place from which he never returned.

To the novice the market looks easy. The movements are rapidly rising or falling a cent in a few minutes' time, therefore why not take out profits with corresponding rapidity? Experience has not yet taught him that the daily movements are the "roulette" of the market and to stake one's all on them is like placing it on the red, black or white space and leaving it to the whirling wheel as to whether he gets a profit or a loss. Unfortunately he will have enough successes to serve as bait for further indulgence. He minimizes his losses and exaggerates his gains, but the spectre of black hooded bad luck will follow him like a shadow until he is forced to quit from lack of funds. Scalping is highly profitable for the broker, for he gets his commission whether the trader loses or wins.

The scalper who plays for a one cent profit must pay the broker one-fourth of his earnings if he wins. The more logical trader who trades for a five cent swing pays the broker only one-twentieth of his earnings. One of the slogans of modern day business is "quick turnover and small profits." Too many traders attempt to carry this practice into the market where it is not operative. It may work at the dime store or at a grocery house, but it's a misfit at the grain market.

Since the Board of Trade was founded at Chicago in 1848 the chief practice of in and out traders has been to capture small profits. It is tempting and always will be. Every new trader who appears at the market place believes his shrewdness will enable him to win where others failed. This is natural and quite human, but the inexorable market will teach him as it has taught others. It is a matter of self-culture that the wise student guard himself against falling into this fascinating but expensive habit where men brush aside the irrevocable laws which govern the market and fall into the habit of idle guesswork.

"PROFESSIONAL TRADERS"

This term, often seen in the newspapers, refers to a few well known market operators whose transactions have been on such a large scale as to bring them into public attention or to make them important figures in the exchanges of the country. Any trader who "gets away with" a big deal successfully is admired and envied by many people. His doings become news. Such operators devote much time to a study of conditions and in learning laws and habits of market action. Most of them dislike publicity, as it prevents them from keeping their market operations secret. When they are deep in a trading campaign they secrete their offices in some hotel or building as remote as possible from the public, in some instances having their rooms unnumbered and not permitting elevator boys or messengers to know their identity. All business is done over the telephone with brokers or others.

The stock market has its list of famous operators of the past and present. Such names as Fiske, Drew, Gould, Vanderbilt, Little, Lawson, Harriman and Keene are widely known in market history. William C. Durant, who operated in the big bull stock market of 1924 to 1929, was said to have eclipsed all of his predecessors in the volume of shares handled.

The grain market has fewer "professionals" to its credit either past or present, but in the colorful days of grain market history will be remembered Leiter of the famous "Leiter corner;" James A. Patten, who became a multi-millionaire trading in wheat and corn; Arthur Cutten, who was a clerk for years in a Chicago brokerage house before coming out as an operator, and Jesse Livermore, known for many years as one of the country's heaviest operators, termed the "greatest bear of all," but fully capable of operating on either side of the market. The last two mentioned are active in the markets at this writing (July, 1932). "Old Hutch" is the sobriquet of a man named Hutchinson who ran a corner in the market in the earlier days, piling up several million dollars only to let it gradually slip through his fingers to the last dollar. Before his death he was selling sandwiches at a shop not far from the Board of Trade.

"SHAKEOUTS" AND "SHORTCOVERING"

These two terms appear so frequently in market news that, for the sake of inexperienced traders a short description is given of how they happen to occur and of their effect upon the market.

"Shakeout" is a market term used when traders holding long grain are forced, by a declining market, to sell out to avoid further loss. Men buy wheat, for instance, believing that it is low enough and due for a rise. They margin their trades several cents and when unexpected events force prices lower they add to margins for awhile until their loss becomes too heavy then they sell out. It is usually supposed that such shakeouts are forced by professional traders who purposely depress the market with a view to buying up the grain that men are forced to sell out. Occasionally such practice may be designed, but natural events cause most of the heavy declines which force longs out of the market. The effect of a shakeout is to cause a break to such a low level that the grain becomes an excellent purchase and other men, more fortunate, rush in and buy. Thus what becomes one man's loss is another man's gain. A very good example of a shakeout is found on page 20, from October 10, 1927, to October 24.

"Shortcovering" is a term used when short sellers have misjudged the market. Thinking it weak, they sell short freely, and when an advance begins to tax their margins they buy in or "cover" their short trades. Thus the name shortcovering. Short sellers are usually far in the minority as compared with the mass of traders. They run to "cover" quickly and are apt to cause very violent upward action as they buy in their lots of grain. A good example of shortcovering is seen on page 20 from the level D where we sent out our "Third wire to buy wheat." The final effect of shortcovering is to run the market up far above just values, making it a target for shotsellers who were not caught by the shortcovering wave. On shortcovering rallies there is always a large number of ill advised buyers who purchase at prices too high and are naturally shaken out later. "Shakeout" means a stiff break. "Shortcovering" a stiff rally.

SPECULATION VS. GAMBLING

This question, long the subject of civic and congressional debate, was answered succinctly by Siebel C. Harris of Chicago in an interview printed by the Associated Press, 1932:

"Gambling is the creation of a risk that does not exist.

"Speculation is the assumption of a risk that does exist.

"Both spring from the eternal inclination of man to take a chance. But the gambler deals with life's artificialities while the speculator trades in the basic commodities of commerce in which, from one cause or another, there is a constant fluctuation of price. This may be due to the whims of Nature in providing a dearth or a plethora of some foodstuff or from the operation of the law of Supply and Demand."

—By Siebel C. Harris, chairman of the National Committee of Grain Exchanges.

BOOK THREE

CRAFTSMANSHIP

It is a pleasure to watch a skilled craftsman work with his tools. He seems to shape the work under his hands with such precision and certainty. He may have dozens of assorted tools, fixtures and attachments, but it will be noticed that he has a favorite few which he depends upon to accomplish the best results. Whether it be the machinist at his lathe, the painter with his canvas, the jeweler, the dentist or the surgeon, each does by far the largest part of his work with the use of a few favored implements. It is even more true in the market place. Skilled traders become skillful not by a multiplicity of tools but by the use of a few select ones that they know will produce results. Some years ago a young man came down from Canada to enter a brokerage house in Chicago as bookkeeper. There he acquired a knowledge of the kind of tools which successful men used on the market. He had ample opportunity to see how the foolish failed and how the wise won. After twelve years careful study he entered the wheat market and, using these successful methods, has now become a national figure in the market world and was said to have acquired, by the palmy days of 1929, a fortune that ran into nine figures.

THE MINOR TREND LINE

One of the few very important tools for use in the grain market is the Minor Trend Line so named because it so often forms a boundary line underneath a minor swing. It is used only in upswings. Downward movements are not nearly so regular as advances and offer no slope or angle that may be bounded by a straight line. The Minor Trend Line is not found in all upswings; only those which show regularity of advance, meaning such advances as are engineered by systematic buyers. It is not necessarily the buying of professional operators that causes a regular advance as it occasionally happens that lesser traders adopt a buying program of purchasing on reactions, each time a little higher than on the previous time down. Note this on the chart, page 5, at the points A-C-D-E.

Big swings are, for the most part, astonishingly regular, though some are so ragged as to offer no basic angle under which to draw a minor trend line and should be left alone. The minor trend line is found both in bull markets and in the big swings that occur in a bear market, hence its extreme usefulness. Almost every month —and sometimes twice a month—a swing will form that may be bounded on the lower side with this line. Perhaps no type of action shown in this course of study is more certain of successful results when followed according to instructions given. In order to acquaint the student with the frequency of this movement a large number of examples are given. Often there is no indication whatever that may be followed except the minor trend line, hence it is highly desirable that it be well understood. When an active wheat market develops following the indication given by KEY NUMBER ONE the next important thing for the trader is to watch for the place to apply the minor trend line. Sometimes he will attempt to draw it too soon and will have to erase it and wait for another day or two of action to determine the proper bottom level. Note this on page 8 of this book at the point G. To have placed the line under point K would be wrong.

3

Since quotations of grain are in eighths of a cent traders think in eighths and it becomes easy to chart the options on paper having rulings one-eighth of an inch apart. Equally good charts may be made by spacing the cent lines one-half cent apart, a style of chart that will take much less chart paper. Also this thinking of prices in eighths has the effect of making the movements conform to certain angles at a time such as that on page 5. A majority of traders thinking in eighths and planning to buy the "next time down" at a little higher level give us the minor trend line.

After a while the profit becomes so alluring that a goodly number of those having long wheat decide to take profits. That destroys the equilibrium of the advance. It turns the majority to the selling side and the price breaks down through the minor trend line as at F on page 5. Of course KEY NUMBER TWO comes into effect this time before the trend line is reached, but many instances will be found in the charts of this course where the minor trend line gave the signal ahead of KEY NUMBER TWO.

Active markets show steeper advances and larger swings. Usually it may be accepted that a steep minor trend line will be followed by a quick, sharp break. Slow swings are mostly short. Often they exhibit very excellent minor trends. From these graphs it will be evident that the minor trend line does not forecast upswings. It is used only to follow up an advance to where it turns for the usual break.

By no means known to the author is it possible to draw a forecasting line either on the upper or lower side of a decline. The "coil" shown in the previous book is the only boundary line that will fit a loose, rambling or declining market and this phenomena is not fully dependable. It will be well for the student to use care and accuracy in making charts of an active option as inaccurate charts might completely defeat his purpose. The style of charts used in this course, showing the open, high, low and close has made it possible for the author to devise the rules and methods of this course.

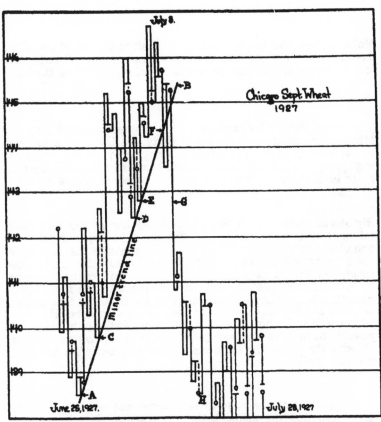

MINOR TREND LINE UNDER SMALL SWING

The line snugly under the lower limits of an eight cent advance in September wheat. While it is a very small upswing it is a clear example of the progressive steps by which a swing often mounts to its top, then breaks down through this trend line making a complete reversal. By means shown in this book and other books in the course it will be possible for the trader to detect the upswing and take a profit by following it up to where it breaks through the minor trend line, then take the down side for another good profit. However, only on the best of indications should the operator try to follow both sides.

HOW TO PLACE THE MINOR TREND LINE

After an advance is several days on the way, draw a line on the underside starting at the lower point as at A.

Let the line touch the bottom of the first reaction as at C. It may be necessary to try two or three times to get the proper first reaction bottom.

5

Not every upswing in grain will adapt itself to the use of the Minor Trend Line. Sometimes an advance that starts out all right falls into irregular action with no semblance of regularity on the lower side.

The Minor Trend Line is more readily adapted to wheat than any other grain owing to its greater activity and the large number of people trading in it. The larger the number of people trading in any grain or stock the better it will conform to market laws because back at the source these laws are based on human nature.

Big stocks such as U. S. Steel have many big swings very easily followed with the Minor Trend. The object of displaying the several charts of the Minor Trend Line is to convince the observer of the genuineness of the line and its usefulness. No matter how firmly the trader may believe the market will continue upward he should not go against the indication given by the minor trend. Various other methods have been given for detecting tops and will be given in later books of this course, but this furnishes the trader with additional proof of a turn in the market. Quite often it is possible to have the advantage of two or three factors, each one showing the top at the same time. Such positions offer the surest possible profits.

In the placing of the line—after a movement starts—it is often discovered that the actual bottom or starting place is not at he extreme bottom of the move but a little higher up. Note on page 14 of this book in the chart of July Corn 1927, that the line should start from the point A, not from the bottom at April 16.

It is essential to remember that while not every upswing will permit the use of the Minor Trend Line, that most of them will and especially the fast, finishing top action of a bull movement right where it does the most good.

SOMETIMES A SINGLE BIG MOVE DEVELOPS TWO MINOR TREND LINES.

6

WHAT CAUSED the advance in the chart on page 4? It was a rally in a bear market. When a bull market is completed a large number of operators, who will not sell short under any circumstances, get out of the market after which it goes into a decline with a battle on between the in and out traders, some of whom are bullish and others bearish. This causes rapid and quite extensive swings many of which conform to the Minor Trend Line and show excellent indications for short sales.

Breaking through the trend line at F means that the advance is virtually finished and the break beginning.

DOES BREAKING THROUGH F invariably indicate top? We may say almost invariably. Instances will be given in this course of "second tops" which exceed the first top and seem to invalidate the minor trend. However these are only a part of the top making process which sometimes covers as much as a month or more.

OF WHAT IMPORTANCE is point C? The rapid rise from there shows that heavy buying stopped the break and operators are expecting to push the market higher. In other words the advance is not over. Again at D and E it is found the market is still being supported.

WHEN THE PRICE BROKE through the Minor Trend Line at F and then closed higher, what did it indicate? Nothing more than a few "eleventh hour" bulls who thinking the advance was over and not understanding the indications, began buying wheat. They paid dearly for their lack-of market knowledge when the big break G occurred.

"ELEVENTH HOUR BULLS" is a term often used in ridicule of those who wait too long before buying into a movement and make the mistake of buying near the top. The author has been through many bull movements and finds that only a small part of the trading public comes into the market during the first third of the advance. The second third finds the public coming in more rapidly while the last third of the advance brings in a big rush of buyers from all walks of life, ranging from bootblacks to bankers. This last stage is the rapid stage which professionals watch for as the place to sell out long grain.

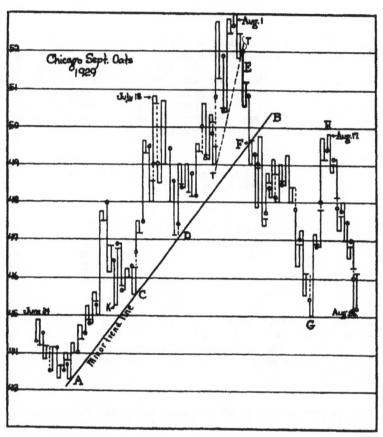

EVEN IN A SMALL GRAIN like oats a steady advance may be bounded by a Minor Trend Line as shown in the chart above. This movement in oats was in sympathy with a bull movement in wheat, the break from August 1st coming at the same time with a break in wheat. While the trend line is of value in confirming the break yet the best results were obtained by KEY NUMBER TWO which showed the top at E.

Again in this chart we have all of the positions that are needed for laying the Minor Trend Line, viz. the points A, C and D.

    A shows where to start the line
    C shows proper reaction against which to lay the line
    D shows a further advance and new highs expected
    E shows top finished and break beginning (KEY 2)
    F confirms the downtrend.

Often a "tip-top" or double trend line occurs. This is seen in the dotted line T - - - T. It is very useful.

8

THE POWER OF PERSISTENCE

A good thing is worth working for. If the business of life is the making of money then the means for making money should be studied with unrelenting persistence. Read again the quotation by Calvin Coolidge on the last page of Book One. The chemist, the mechanic and the surgeon spend years of meticulous study in the perfecting of their professions and yet the only object of their study is to make money. If the trader is in earnest and wishes earnestly to make money out of his market transactions he must take the time and thought necessary to perfect his knowledge of market action and market laws. It is a fact patent to any one that hit and miss trading very soon puts the trader "down and out." Charts should be kept as carefully as an accountant would keep up his ledger.

The critics of chart making are many. The real reason for their objection is their indolence. The best traders in the country use them profusely. It does not follow that any one who will make careful charts of the options will succeed. He must operate according to the laws and habits native to market action. The exchanges are full of chart makers who watch the surface only and seem never to delve down to find the laws which govern the action. The trader must know what is ABOUT TO TAKE PLACE.

IN THAT OATS MOVEMENT on page 8 our student trader would know by the time the price got to 46 that a much further advance was to be seen. He would buy oats. At point D he would be reassured of higher prices but at E he would sell out all long oats and sell short for a break. With Key No. 2 showing him the top day and with the "tip-top" trend line T - - - T assisting he would take almost full profits for the advance and would immediately sell short knowing that the break through the minor trend line at F was sure to follow because two other indications had already made good.

Still another top indication is given in BOOK FIVE and there are many instances when the student will find three separate factors uniting to show the top of a movement.

9

CAN YOU KEEP LEVEL?

Most people are swayed too easily by market action, especially if they are watching the quotation board.

When a person is seen who readily moves from a bearish to a bullish opinion it may be set down as a certainty that he is not doing his own thinking. Perhaps not thinking at all.

Vacillating persons have nothing definite to hold to. They are unaware of market laws or profess contempt for them. The effort to analyze market action is too troublesome for them. They comfort themselves with the belief that all markets are a pure matter of chance and guesswork, little different from tossing dice.

If there were not market laws there would be no professional traders, no millionaires made by the market, no big operators or outstanding personalities incident to the grain business. Every wealthy operator was once a small trader who set himself to the task of learning market action.

When times of confusion beset the trader he should run back carefully through all indications he has at hand. He should compare his charts to find the action of similar movements. When the hunter becomes lost in dense woods his first effort is to locate the direction. He examines the side of trees having the thickest bark or the most moss, knowing that moss is thicker and bark heavier on the north side. Or he may watch the migration of fowls in their northward flight, he thus analyzes his position—or trend—and sets out for his destination.

If you can watch rapidly mounting quotations without being drawn irresistibly into the market; if you can hear the excited talk of traders and pass it by with a smile; if you can wait confidently while the market takes its time in disclosing a definite trend; if you can buy five thousand bushels when you have ample money for twenty thousand bushels and can take profits before you think the top is reached you are of the stuff that makes success and you may look forward to days of pleasure and wealth.

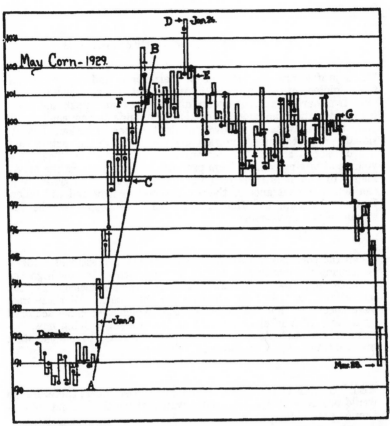

AN EARLY SPRING ADVANCE of May Corn, 1929, furnishes an excellent example of a corn movement that could be forecast by KEY NUMBER ONE and confirmed by the use of the Minor Trend Line.

First —The start of the advance was clearly forecast by the use of KEY NO. 1.

Second—The top was plainly shown by KEY NO. 2 at the point F.

Third —The decline was confirmed when the price broke below the point F.

This advance in corn was apparently engineered by skillful operators. All through December, previous to the rise, this option had moved in a narrow range denoting "accumulation." Bullish crop news from Argentine was sufficient to excite a rush of buying. The sharp rise of Jan. 9 sent the price well above the bottom congestion and corn became a purchase at the market. Market keys are few but they are immensely important.

11

IN THE FOOTSTEPS OF PROFESSIONALS

When professional traders throw their funds and the weight of their opinion into the market the movements become easier to follow. If a market is about evenly divided between bullish and bearish opinion then the sudden addition of outside or new capital will almost certainly cause a powerful drift in **one direction.** Professionals prefer to enter a market after a period of dull action that has developed around the bottom levels of a decline. The extra volume of buying coming from professionals often starts the movement. In fact it is their purpose that it should. The trader who can detect the entrance of the professional element and will follow in their footsteps will find trading easy and simple for the full extent of the movement.

When the corn movement started (page 11) professional traders, sponsoring the movement, had no definite idea as to how high the advance might be carried but relied upon their knowledge of "top indications" to tell them when to sell their corn. All these men have special methods of detecting tops which they have acquired by a study of market action just as the student is doing now.
If one of our students were following this movement from the start his reasoning would be about as follows:

KEY NO. ONE shows accumulation during December; therefore, he would buy corn on the two cent advance above the bottom congestion or around 94.

He would watch for the first important reaction as a place against which to lay the minor trend line for future use.

When the advance continued above the point C he would watch for the first break—applying KEY NO. TWO—and would sell out either on that key day or when the price broke below the Minor Trend Line as at F.

He would either sell short at once or on the next rally around 102 or 103 knowing that the decline would eventually work back to the starting place 94.

12

The rally to D in the corn chart on page 11 is nothing more than the "second top." It is more often seen in wheat but may occur in any grain or any stock. While the second top is not always forecastable, it does not alter the fact that the market is making top. In this chart it is seen that two top days are used. The first one was sufficient at F but the second one at E gave additional confirmation,

A very unusual feature appears in this chart in the protracted time of "distribution" from F to E. It is customary market action for a sharp topped bull movement to revert at once into a rapid decline. In this case more than a month of desultory daily action took place before the final break to March 28 occurred. Such periods offer many opportunities for the in and out trader. If he understands market law he will sell on these rallies and take profits on the breaks but will stay carefully away from the long side after the top signal is given. By this time the student has learned that a vertical rise, such as that shown in the corn chart, places the market at a "strain" and the price will be pulled back down again. For that reason every new commitment should be a sale after the top at F. TWO BIG PROFITS were available to the skillful trader in this corn move which began on January 9 and ended March 28, ten weeks later, and it is highly probable that far larger profits would be made in this way than by the most careful in-and-out trading. With KEY NUMBER ONE the trader would make his initial purchase around 94 and would carry his trade up to at least to 101. There he would sell short and prepare to buy in at 91. The round trip would be made in ten weeks with a double profit and he could double his lot on both the upward trip and the downward trip. In this particular chart the trader will observe a very unusual phenomena in the top congestion lasting from F to G. Only rarely do narrow congestions form at the top of an advance. Narrow, dull markets are found, nine times out of ten, at the bottom of a decline, but knowing the simple laws of market action our student trader is able to follow the price in both directions. It is important to remember that there are only two major trends, up and down, and that the market is always in one or the other.

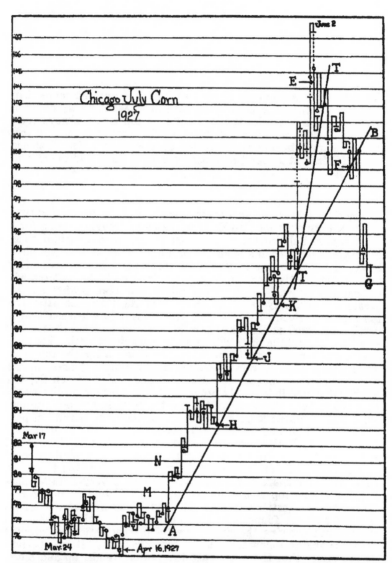

Chicago July Corn
1927

"TALL TREES from little acorns grow" runs the schoolboy's ballad, and the same idea applied to grains would be "bull moves from little movements grow." In the corn chart above is a very brilliant example of how small movements starting at the bottom of a decline can result in a tremendous advance. Other useful things, in the line of forecasting, develop in such an advance. You have the minor trend line, the tip-top line (T - - - T), KEY NUMBER ONE to start with at the bottom and KEY NUMBER TWO to detect the top at E. Thus the trader has full equipment with which to follow this movement to the end.

14

CHARTS ARE MARKET MIRRORS

The charts of this course furnish the trader with a storehouse of information for future use. Herein is found most of the bull and bear markets and the principal types of action for a period of ten years back. By inspecting one chart you see the probable outline of the next bull movement or bear movement. Even if there were no explanatory text these faithfully charted markets would be worth the price of the course and more. Market action is human habits photographed. It is correct market history in keen detail. It is a map, a guide as indispensable to the trader as a compass is to the mariner on the seas. To the market student it is **proof.**

What a beautiful play was that afforded by corn back there in the middle of 1927. Dry weather was the exciting cause. June and July are the critical months for the new corn crop and are responsible for the starting of more bull movements than any other months in the year. Our student trader, watching this movement at its inception, would have bought corn by KEY NUMBER ONE, followed it by the Minor Trend Line, watched the weather for outside indications and would have taken profits by selling out at E on KEY NUMBER TWO. It's not at all difficult. You can see it easily with the charted movement before you but you couldn't begin to visualize such a market except by the **use of a chart.**

The "Tip-Top" trend line comes into play here and is very useful. It is quite frequent. Perhaps four out of five bull market tops are finished with the Tip-Top line. Occasionally a big swing—not a bull market top—will develop a tip-top trend line which is nothing more than a top story for the regular Minor Trend Line. (Note T - - - T, page 17). Up to the present the student has acquired only a few Keys and laws of the market but they are par-excellent. They will fit many of the largest movements known to the grain market. Other forecasting methods of increasing value will be shown in the succeeding books of this course. Each new one adds to the student's market knowledge and to his equipment for extracting profits from the market. Quality, not quantity, of information is the essential factor of success in the grain market.

IS PYRAMIDING SAFE?

It is in genuine bull movements and may, also, be used in bear movements, but in the latter it is likely to cause concern to the trader because of the big rallies that occur in bear movements. In the corn move on page 14 the trader has abundant evidence on the advance between A and H that some very high prices are to be seen. The first lot would be bought between M and N, say around 80. And another lot above H where the market crosses 85 and, again, at J or K. Wheat, bought at these different levels, can be held for fast action which does not develop until above the point T. All of this grain should be held until the point E is reached, thus enabling the trader to take a very large profit.

Pyramiding is often made top-heavy by purchases of wheat in increasing size lots. For instance, five thousand bushels would be bought at 80, ten thousand at 85, fifteen thousand around J and twenty thousand around K. This is a dangerous procedure as a very small break would consume all of the profits made and not every bull market runs through with the precision of the movement on page 14.

The proper way to pyramid is to take a rather heavy lot at 80, then make each of the succeeding lots the same size or less. Then the pyramid has the big end down while the other way has the big end up. It would be a difficult matter for the trader to adhere to a conservative program and not overload as a steadily advancing market breeds over-confidence and he is likely to build his air castles on too grand a scale.

The chief thing to observe, when a market is being pyramided, is the top signal. When fast action develops at the top of a bull market it is more than likely that a secondary minor trend line or tip-top trend line will develop as shown at T - - - T. That line is a signal that the movement is about over and that the long wheat pyramided on the way up must be sold out. You have, in this case, KEY NUMBER TWO and the Tip-Top trend line to show you when to unload your long grain, and there should be no hesitancy in selling out. Hanging on for a little more has ruined many a trader.

16

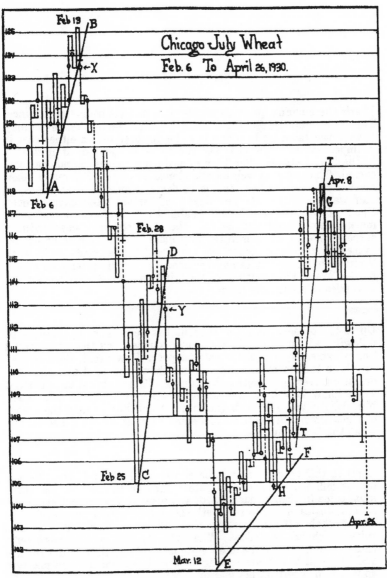

Chicago July Wheat
Feb. 6 To April 26, 1930.

THREE MINOR TREND LINES IN 60 DAYS offered traders an extra run
of profits in wheat during the spring of 1930 in July wheat. Perhaps very
few secured such profits as the Minor Trend Line is original with the author
and is only in this course fully displayed to market students. Occasionally
this line appears in rapid succession as shown above in the bear market of
wheat. One big swing is of such aggressiveness that a tip-top trend line
develops at T - - - T.

"HOW HIGH?"

That's the burning question whenever a market begins to advance. The trader may be seeking a place to enter the market or he may have a profitable trade which is to be disposed of. In either case it is important to know how far the move is spent or if it is just in the initial stages. The tops of ordinary swings cannot be forecasted. That may as well be abandoned at once. For many years market people have been trying to devise a system of averages, or half way reactions, of "key days," of certain week days or even times of the day which will enable them to forecast the small market movements but, so far, their efforts have been without success. We must, therefore, stay close to the sources or deeper causes of market action. "The boy's will is the wind's will," says Whittier in one of his famous poems. The small movements of the market are as irresponsible as the wind and will deceive the person who tries to anticipate them.

Up to the present time the student has been learning methods of following advances on their upward journey and the minor trend line is extremely useful for this purpose. However, it does not tell how high the movement is going but shows the point at which it is definitely over and a decline beginning. This is almost as important as to know how high the advance will go because with KEY NUMBER TWO and with the minor trend line to help the trader can get almost the entire movement **without** knowing beforehand what the top should be.

Later in this course you will be shown methods of forecasting the top of bull movements long before the top is reached, but these must come in their order and for the present the student should be content to learn the lesser methods of forecasting with a view to adding their effectiveness to the still more important laws and rules which are to follow. When the student gets through with this course he should have an equipment that will last him for life and that will be a never ending source of convenience and pleasure as well as of profit in his market work.

WHAT THE MINOR TREND LINE TELLS

Positive knowledge in market affairs is of a measureable value because it can be used throughout the life of the trader. The things learned in this course will never be forgotten. They become to the student what the saw is to the carpenter, the scalpel to the surgeon, the transit to the surveyor, or the compass to the mariner. Condensed into brief sentences the minor trend line, one of the new tools which our reader can adopt, renders aid in the following manner:

Starting not far from the bottom it furnishes the first real evidence that a sustained advance is in progress.
By serving as a resting place for reactions such as are shown at H-J-K the trader knows that the market is yet to go much higher. It does not tell how high an advance will go but it does tell when the move will go no higher.

It tells when to sell out long grain and when to sell the market short. When it develops into a long and persistent line, covering several weeks, it tells the trader that a bull market is in progress and that it may finish with a tip-top line which is merely a second story to the minor trend line.

If the student is doubtful that this line will "work" he needs but refer back to the large number of different examples shown in this book and he will be reassured. It is often difficult for the amateur to believe that a given market law demonstrated in the chart will work for the particular market in which he is operating. Even the experienced trader becomes doubtful and the reason is because he tries so many minor schemes for forecasting the market which fail that he falls into the habit of doubting all market methods. However, we have yet to see the man who will quit the market because of erring methods or from his own mistakes. He still blunders on.

19

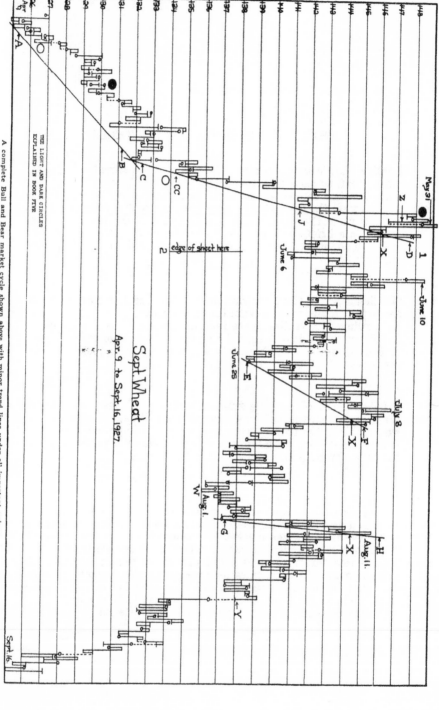

Sept. Wheat

Apr. 9 to Sept. 16, 1927.

THE LIGHT AND DARK CIRCLES
EXPLAINED IN BOOK FIVE

A complete Bull and Bear market cycle shown above with minor trend lines under all important swings.

RIPE FOR A PROFIT

The big wheat movement spread before the trader on pages 20 and 21 shows the marvelous opportunity for profits which develops in one of these cycle movements by which we mean a complete round trip of the price from bottom to top and back again. Here the student trader has the chance to test his money making powers to the limit. While the chart is a picture of the market after "it's all over," yet it is very similar to all such movements in its different parts.

By referring back to Book II, page 6, the reader will see the earlier beginnings of this same movement and that it is forecastable from the start by the use of KEY NUMBER ONE.

Now by looking over the many charts of big movements shown in these books it will be seen that the smallest of them was 23 cents. Most of them were 30 to 50 cents in extent, therefore, from the outset the trader knows that with the rising market once above the bottom congestion and KEY NUMBER ONE effective he will get an advance of at least 23 cents and perhaps much more. He can buy heavily but should never tax his margins, a mistake that may be fatal even in a bull movement.

The minor trend lines will not tell how high the top may be but plain reasoning will tell the trader that it should be at least 23 cents up from the bottom as that is the smallest bull movement recorded in ten years. The Minor Trend Line tells when the advance is over no matter how brief or how extensive the movement has been. Take the line C-D and note how nearly it announces the top. When the price broke through that line at X the trader knew positively that the bull movement was over and further progress in these books will show him that it was over for many months to come.

The small black and white circles are explained in Book V and we may add that this course will increase in interest and usefulness of methods to the last page. The aim has been to display and discuss the simpler things first.

TAKE BIG PROFITS

It is more in the nature of big business and of successful deals that the trader take a large profit rather than to attempt a series of small profits by in and out trading. Large operators may wait a year or even two years for the kind of action which forecasts a big movement. Very few professional traders are interested in the small movements or even the considerable swings but they are past masters in their profession when a bull market begins to take form. In the movement on page 21 the student trader would buy his first lot of wheat around 1.30 which would be two cents above the bottom of the congestion as shown in a previous chart. He would buy a second lot at 1.35 after he sees the market beginning its fast, finishing rise. Thus he would take a sixteen cent profit on the first lot and an eleven cent profit on the second lot when he sold out the entire line at 1.46 where the price goes through the trend line at X.

That would be a very handsome profit and much more than can be obtained by attempting to buy on the small reactions and sell out on the rallies. In a later book we will show you, by the actual trading experience of large operators in a bull market, that they will often make serious blunders and will fail to get the full move even though they get in right at the start. The reason is because they understand only a part of the laws of a bull movement. In your later studies as you go through this course it will be well to refer frequently to this very remarkable movement complete from beginning to end shown on pages 20 and 21. We cannot tell you all of the features which attend this movement because they are reserved for a more detailed explanation in Books V and VI. The chief object in displaying this chart at the present time is because of its numerous minor trend lines. First these lines come into operation very usefully on the advance where they practically forecast the full movement. Then after the bull movement is finished they come into play for detecting secondary declines from the big swing as shown at E-F and also at G-H.

MAKE HAY IN SUNNY WEATHER

In the market "make hay" when movements are active. The sharpest activity develops at high prices. Sustained activity, day after day, occurs at times when the market has recently gone through a big convulsive movement such as the bull movement shown on page 20. Such activity will prove a veritable harvest for the student trader who operates along the plans described in this course, that is, by the use of market law. As soon as he has taken his profit from the bull movement he should at once reverse his position, convert his sentiments from bullish to bearish ideas and begin an active campaign on the down side because the bear market activities, which begin at once after the top of a bull move, will afford an excellent opportunity for a profit on the down side but always with danger should the trader resume the buying side. One of the chief faults of traders who do not understand market law is the resuming of buying operations on the first good sized reaction under the belief that the advance is about to be continued.

As a means of illustrating the general ignorance of market law we may state that in our daily market service we find that very few new subscribers come in during the early stages of a bull movement. By the time the move is half over they begin to subscribe freely up until the last day of the movement but the heaviest rush of subscriptions arrives after the bear market begins. Thus most of the traders miss the good movement and get in at the eleventh hour around top figures and then become anxious when the market begins to go against them. If they could see how these laws work in the market they would buy when prices are low, sell out when prices are high and toppling and take the short side with the first important break as shown by KEY NUMBER TWO. This is scientific trading and will be profitable in the extreme for the trader who can and will hold himself to such a trading program. Fortunately the keys, laws and methods usable to forecast market action are very few. Also they are comparatively simple and easily followed when laid out flat and plain before the student, as shown in the numerous charts of this course .

24

THE MULTI-PROFIT PLAN

Getting the most out of the market is a much cherished desire of
the trader. As success begins to attend his efforts his eagerness
to cash in on all movements increases and he falls into the dangerous habit of playing the market both ways, something which, in
the author's opinion, cannot be done successfully or for very long.
In order to satisfy the demand for a plan of trading which may be
followed continually during the long, slow, declining period of a
bear market, the author has devised a plan of trading which because
of the frequency of profits, is termed the "Multi-Profit Plan."   It
is not used in a bull market because a one-way movement should be
followed with trades which are held through to the end, therefore,
the "Multi-Profit Plan" comes into use more specifically at the
beginning of a bear market. Referring to the chart on page 20 the
bear market began "officially" at X when wheat stood at 1.46.
From then on until the point Y is reached, a period of nearly three
months, a large number of violent fluctuations took place which
would yield handsomely in an organized plan of procedure. Most
traders have no organized plan and in attempting to follow a series
of swings will be caught on the wrong side so often that they will
lose all they make in their successful trades. Not understanding
the nature of these rapid movements men try to trade in and out
until finally they give up in disgust, resolving to stand aside and
wait for the next bull move. This may be a long time coming and
they would lose valuable time and many nice profits.

By adopting the "Multi-Profit Plan" a large number of moderate
profits may be taken as will be described on the following page.
This, of course, is more intensive market work and must be followed
with great concentration. If the trader is not adapted to a campaign
of active trading he should not use this method but if he wants to
be in the market all the time and not lose that very valuable and
sometimes extensive period which follows a bull market top he can
take up the "Multi-Profit Plan" with success and with very excellent profits.

Since most bull markets run their course in six weeks and spend three to five months in bear market movements this multi-profit plan best fits a bear market. Even the long, slow bull markets are followed by slow bear markets. Condensing a program of trading into a pair of short sentences the following plan may be suggested:

BUY INTO A BULL MOVEMENT AS NEAR THE BOT-TOM AS POSSIBLE AND HOLD FOR THE TOP.

SELL SHORT WHEN A BEAR MARKET STARTS AND FOLLOW THE MULTI-PROFIT PLAN TO THE BOT-TOM.

Of course, for those who do not wish to carry on an extensive or concentrated market campaign, a short sale should be made when the Minor Trend Line is broken and the trade held through for the bottom.

The Multi-Profit Plan is intensive. It is capable of yielding astonishing profits but like any other policy of business it must be strictly adhered to. It cannot be used for a few days, then sidetracked for the next few days. Therefore, assuming that the student is willing to be on tip-toe for fast action and rapid trading, we will take a trip through the extremely active bear market which followed the bull market top May 31, 1927. This is commonly called the "distribution" period or that period during which professional traders sell out to the "public" which has little or no knowledge of market laws and never takes the time to learn them. Those who are ignorant of market action are always at a disadvantage with those who know.

Seldom does a bear market go straight back down to the starting point. It may set out with a fast break, as may be noted on page 20 from May 31 to June 6, but "distribution" is effected with many sharp breaks and rallies. Starting from the top day and counting the cent lines crossed, it will be found that from 31 to the point Y September wheat passed over a total of 143 cents. Of course, it is not possible for any scheme of trading to secure all of these profits but the Multi-Profit Plan comes the nearest of any method known as the student will see.

MULTI-PROFIT PLAN IN OPERATION

Place a sheet of paper over the right hand part of the chart on page 20 with the left edge of the sheet at the figures 1-2 as shown. Now draw the sheet to the right slowly uncovering each day's movement from June 6th on.

Bacause of the probability of the "double top" described previously it is assumed that the student trader has taken a profit on the drop to June 6. The plan now is to SELL ON A TWO CENT SCALE UP AND ACCEPT A TWO CENT PROFIT ON EACH AND EVERY SALE. That is, place an order with your broker to sell a lot on each two cent advance (open order) and as soon as each sale is confirmed by the broker give him an immediate open order to buy in two cents lower. You may accumulate several lots on a scale up so be careful not to use lots larger than can be well margined. 20 cents per bushel on each lot should be used. However after the "double top" has been made (June 10) and the market is on down grade again trades are comparatively safe margined at 1.50. Follow this trading scheme through. It is intensely interesting.

From June 6 to June 10 using 5000 bushel lots:

Trader sells short.   Takes profits.
5000 bu. at........1.43
5000 bu. at........1.45.........Buys in at........1.43
5000 bu. at........1.47........Buys in at 1.45
        (Proift on the 1.43 lots comes later)

On other rallies and breaks from June 10 to June 25:

Sells 5000 bu. at........1.45 and buys in at........1.43
Sells 5000 bu. at....... .1.45 and buys in at.......1.43
Now buys in the 1.43 lot (note above) at..........1.41

Keep drawing the sheet of paper slowly to the right uncovering the daily movements. Thus you keep the movements hidden just as if trading in a real market. In learning to follow this movement you are learning to follow the one which is yet to be made.

Having now closed all trades and with a two cent profit for each one the operator now waits for fresh action and on the rally from E

Sells 5000 bu. at......1.41.........buys in at......1.39
Sells 5000 bu. at......1.43.........buys in at 1.41
Sells 5000 bu. at......1.45.........buys in at 1.43
Sells 5000 bu. at......1.45.........buys in at 1.43
Sells 5000 bu. at .....1.45.........buys in at 1.43
Sells 5000 bu. at .....1.40.........buys in at......1.38
Sells 5000 bu. at......1.40.........buys in at......1.38

From observing the above method it is noted that no sale is made except on a two cent advance from any bottom. Also for convenience the cent lines are used, not halves or quarters of a cent as 1.45½, etc.

The minor trend line from E to F offers a fine opportunity to take a bigger profit and it is within the bounds of market law to hold the lots for a full break to the bottom levels of June 25.

By following the further movements of the market from W to H the trader takes six more lots and on the break to Y clears out all trades with a profit making a total of **eighteen successful deals** and every one safely within the limits of market action and market law. The total profits would be 36 cents on 5000 bushels or $1,800, less commissions.

At all times the student trader may know he is following the market correctly, in this Multi-Profit Plan, because all of the sharp advances to a bull market top and the subsequent breaking of the Minor Trend Line show the price will—according to bear market law—break back to approximately the starting point as shown at the level reached Sept. 16.

The slow trader, not using the Multi-Profit Plan, would have sold short at X (after May 31) and other lots on a scale down but the rally from Aug. 1 to Aug. 11 would have disturbed him considerably. However either plan is correct and profitable. It depends upon the wishes of the individual.

NINETY PERCENT PREFER THE BUYING SIDE

Most people prefer the long side of the market. Some persons are, in fact, of the opinion that short selling is morally wrong and not constructive. An old market adage with plenty of jingle but no reason runs as follows:

> "He who sells what isn't his'n
> Must pay the price or go to pris'n."

Often this is quoted as a slap at short sellers but it is not only futile but foolish. When considered intelligently it must be seen that short selling is the other half of the market. The contractor who bids on a bridge or a skyscraper is a short seller. The shipyard which offers to build a ship for Uncle Sam for ten million dollars is selling something it does not have nor does it own the materials.

But laying aside all argument the vast majority of our population is happier when prices are advancing. Almost everybody has property of some sort that is more valuable when prices are advancing. When the stock market is advancing by rapid strides the exchanges will be filled with happy excited men. When the market is breaking the exchanges are mostly empty and the few men present look disappointed and blue.

The skillful trader is the one who is not "married" to either side of the market but leaves himself open to market conditions and ready to reverse with the trend at any time. One side of the market is just as useful in making profits as the other and often it happens that the bear market is drawn out much longer than the bull market. To follow one side only is to be limited by prejudice that costs the loss of much valuable time and many fine profits. Arthur Cutten is considered as favoring the bull side and Jesse Livermore the bear side yet each is known to have operated successfully on either side. If they follow a bull market up they usually follow the bear market down as will be shown later in this course.

29

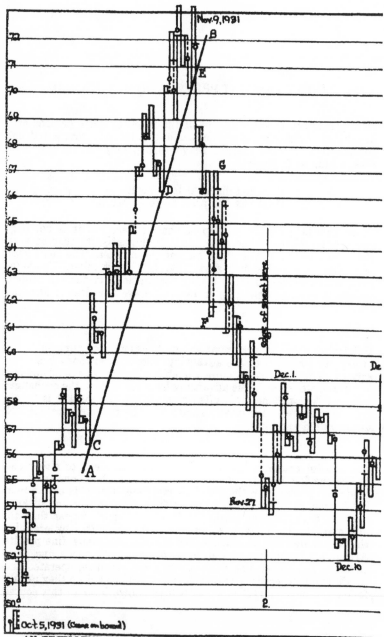

Nov.9,1931

B

E

D

G

F

Signs of sharp Move

De

Dec.1

Nov.27

Dec.10

C

A

2.

Oct 5,1931 (Close on board)

AN EXCELLENT EXAMPLE of the Minor Trend Line occurs in the short,
quick bull move in wheat beginning Oct. 5 and ending Nov. 5, 1931. The steep
rise of 24½ cents was made in 34 days and under the lower side of this advance appears the faithful Minor Trend Line.

30

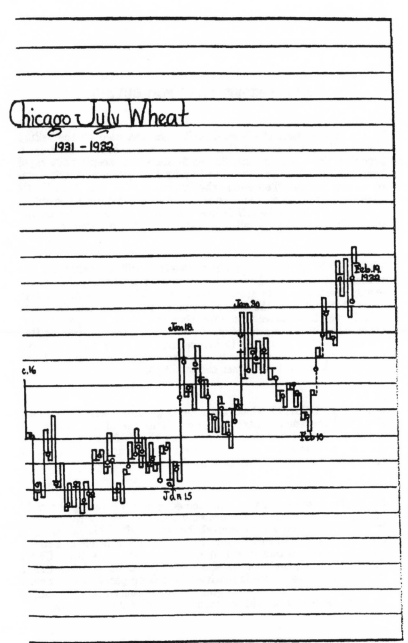

Chicago July Wheat
1931 - 1932

c. 16

Jan 15

Jan 18.

Jan 30

Feb 10

Feb 19
1932

THIS REMARKABLE ACTION of wheat, starting on the opposite page October 5, 1931, continued far past Feb. 19. It ran on until July 19, 1932 when the price again slumped down to the low level of October making a "double bottom" for the depression period about nine months apart.

MULTI-PROFIT PLAN FOR BUYING

In a previous chart the Multi-Profit Plan was used on the selling side which is the correct thing to do when a bear market is in progress. The chart on pages 30 and 31 shows an exceptionally rapid bear market which ran down so low by Dec. 10 as to nearly complete the decline. Therefore, the trader applies the Multi-Profit Plan to the buying side and he need not even wait until December. The price by November 27 is low enough to begin trading on the long side only. That is, all new commitments are purchases.

WHY DOES WHEAT DRIFT "sidewise" will be asked by the student. It is a period of confused opinion with the public about evenly divided on both sides. Wheat is waiting for some event to come that will turn the tide of opinion strongly in one direction. Usually the turn comes from crop shortage in the U. S. or in some other large exporting country. In this case wheat prices drifted for nine months or to July 18 before the turn came, following crop damage reported from Canada but also helped by a sudden boom in the stock market and other commodities.

Beginning at Nov. 27 wheat movements go into a series of undulations that precede the next bull move. This period may last a few weeks or several months. Seldom does the drifting bear market continue as long as the present example which was far too extensive to place on a chart showing each day's action.

By placing a sheet of paper with the edge at 1-2 covering the right hand part of the chart, then drawing the sheet slowly to the right it will be seen that a very remarkable series of purchases could be made by the Multi-Profit Plan. But at these low levels and consequently narrow action wheat should be bought on a ONE CENT SCALE DOWN, and profits should be taken on a TWO CENT SCALE UP. The trader is justified in making purchases this close together and is safe as to margins which, of course, must be ample. In this case wheat should be margined to 40 for every trade.

WHERE THE TRAINED TRADER WINS

Training one's self to believe in market laws and to use them with confidence is somewhat difficult at first as the trader hears so many outside opinions—based upon whim, not thought—which disturb him or cause him to doubt. The writing of this set of books covered the entire time from October, 1931, to the bull movement in the fall of 1932 or nearly a full year. During that time the author was in constant communication with subscribers to his service as well as in contact with traders at the exchanges. Less than one percent of the entire number had any distinct idea of market laws or market action. When a bull movement started not one was well enough versed in bull market habits to hold to grain, sometimes well bought, for even the first small stage of the advance. The inclination was to "sell out and try to buy again cheaper." It is this ignorance of bull markets that makes the advances so strong. Those who sell out "to buy cheaper" finally rush in to buy on an advance instead. Also a few deluded traders sell short and are forced to "cover" as the price goes irresistibly upward. Finally when the price is high and rising by leaps and bounds the whole mass of the trading public begins buying "at the market" and finds that these purchases are around top prices.

The trained trader avoids the very things that make the others fail. First of all, he remembers that he must know the trend. He charts the market from which he expects to take money. It pays to do anything well. He uses margins that are certain to be adequate. This for his comfort as well as his financial safety. He runs through the different types of movements (as charted in this course) and by applying the rules and methods learned decides whether the market should be sold or bought or if the Multi-Profit Plan should be used. When trading actively he keeps away from others who scatter free opinions relying solely upon the proven actions of the market as his guide. He does not expect to be a wizard or do impossible things but simply to make a business matter out of his market work.

33

TAKING REAL MONEY FROM THE MARKET

The money you make in the market is just as real as the gold in the United States Treasury yet you often hear it said somewhat contemptuously that the trader's "paper profits" in a certain deal amounted to such a sum. The so-called paper profits will be real whenever the trader completes his trade. If he buys wheat at 50 cents and sells it at 60 cents his paper profits become real profits. The money taken from a deal in wheat is as genuine as the money taken in the sale of real estate or merchandise. Perhaps whatever criticism is aimed at paper profits is the failure of traders to take said profits, which—by the way—is one of the sad human failings. After having had a very excellent profit the trader lets his deal run into a loss and accepts the loss where he will not accept the profit.

A policy for taking profits by organized methods is given the student in the Multi-Profit Plan. One of the very useful features of this method is the fact that it establishes a definite profit-taking place for every trade. It is not left to the whim of the trader but orders are placed with the broker in advance and thus taken out of the hands of the trader. The other means of making money by following a bull movement through to the end and by waiting for KEY NUMBER TWO, or the Minor Trend Line, to show the completion of the deal are just as orderly and as definite as the Multi-Profit Plan, only the trades run longer. The important point is that the student trader should decisively and positively accept his profits when the market shows that the time has arrived. It is fatal to success to hold on to a trade which has run its course waiting to see if by some unexpected turn of luck still more profit will not accrue. The wheat market or stock market makes money for the successful trader as positively and as willingly as merchandising makes money for the successful merchant. It is a matter of operating skillfully in either business. One of the greatest difficulties for the amateur trader is to convince himself that the market is not a simple affair but that it demands his keenest attention if success is to be won.

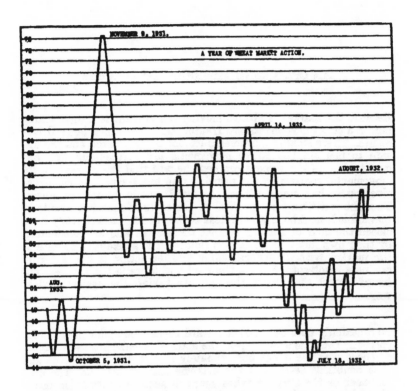

A YEAR OF WHEAT MARKET ACTION.

NOVEMBER 9, 1931.

APRIL 14, 1932.

AUGUST, 1932.

AUG. 1931

OCTOBER 5, 1931.

JULY 18, 1932.

HOW WHEAT MADE BOTTOM during the year of the big depression is shown in the chart above which covers an entire year from August, 1931 to August, 1932, during which time wheat made a bottom between 44 and 45, October 5 and reached practically the same figure the next time July 18, 1932, thus making a double bottom for the great bear market in wheat. During this year period wheat had a small bull market topping out November 9, 1931. After that came eight months of very active swings, common to a bear market, finally making bottom the second time in July. This very graphically illustrates the bear market law which will be elaborated on in Book Six. During this long period the Multi-Profit Plan could have been used to great advantage, also several of the big swings showed excellent minor trend lines. The advance beginning July 18 finally carried the price above the bottom congestion (at 53¼) which indicates the beginning of a much further advance. This chart shows the final contortions of the wheat market in finishing full liquidation and starting a new economic uptrend.

AN OPEN MIND THE DOOR TO SUCCESS

Because the market is always moving the student is always learning. All small movements are fragmentary parts of a large movements. These smaller movements cannot be forecasted and are unsafe to use but the larger movements are forecastable and are profitable. As the student proceeds he will find the market, in its movements, confirming the principles he has learned. A constructive course has many critics. Languid minds prefer to guess. Thought is difficult but profitable. Guessing is easy but results in inevitable loss. Those who profess contempt for market study have closed the door of success against themselves and are condemned by their own indolence to certain failure. The attempt to operate in the market without understanding market action is like entering business insolvent. Wide is the road and large is the restless, unhappy crowd that drifts through life taking the easiest, laziest way.

So amazingly does the market reward those who make their trades correctly that one would expect the market to make intense students of those who use it but unfortunately this is not always true and it is doubtless because of the extreme ease of trading. The civil engineer or the surgeon takes years to acquire exact information about his profession and his sole purpose is to make money just as the purpose of the wheat trader is to make money. If market operators would interest themselves as deeply in learning the laws of the market they would be as successful as the engineer and the surgeon.

The author would say to his readers: ignore the reams of idle opinion found in newspapers and written by men who get so much per week. Keep in line with the market by studying its action. Chart the options that you may have a perfect likeness of market action. Prices are made by thought. Advancing prices indicate a bullish majority and the composite opinion of men is correct. It may be said briefly: Individual opinion is indispensable but the combined opinion of the majority is correct.

MAKE GRAIN TRADING A SIDELINE

Stick to your job or your business. The object of these books is not to induce anyone to drop their business and go into grain speculation but to make the most out of their deals when they do speculate. Grain trading has an irresistible fascination which is difficult to overcome when once the taste is acquired and since this is true the best defense is to acquire market knowledge so keen that you can make your grain trading pay. Otherwise the habit will be expensive and will cause you loss instead of paying.

Your job or your business is a good balance wheel. It teaches you to exercise judgment, to plan, to organize, to command workers, to understand values and how to expand business. The best traders are men who do not leave their business to trade but who give their orders over the telephone. Anyone can find out what's doing in the market without visiting the exchange.

To adopt speculation as a business narrows your activities down to the market only and will in time limit your interest to market news and market prices and may carry you into the very limited range of opinions prevalent at the brokerage house. It is possible to trade in large quantities of wheat without visiting the exchange. The reader of these lessons may be surprised to know that there are active traders in almost every town in the country including the thinly populated grain sections of the southwest. They keep posted with a daily grain service letter and do their trading by telephone.

Well known to the author is a successful trader living in a good sized town sixty miles from any exchange. He is a well-to-do merchant, interested in civic affairs, a director in two banks, interested in educational institutions and has a large business which he owns outright. He has a great fondness for trading and acquires much pleasure from forcing the market to yield him a recompense and is able to fit himself to the trend of the market whether it be up or down. He buys wheat or stocks, although he prefers wheat and he makes money on all of them.

One of the desirable faculties of this man is his ability to take profits. He does not worry when the market is against him because he uses margins that will hold his trades. Neither does he become fidgety and snap off small profits. He waits for a fair profit, then takes it. His three-fold ability is his knowledge of market action, his ability to margin his trades fully and last, but not least, his faculty for taking profits.

Another incident known to the author shows keen business judgment. A man in the thirties got into a big move during the early stages of the great war. With $250 he pyramided successfully and eventually piled up a profit of $80,000. He was an amateur but became a little inflated over his success. He determined to go ahead and make a million but he loaded up a little too heavily and lost $20,000 in a quick break of the market. He paused to catch his breath and to reflect on the dangers of over-trading. Taking the $60,000 left he bought a new home and deeded it to his wife, then bought other real estate and reserved $10,000 in cash for his speculative ventures, being determined to make a closer study of the market and to jeopardize only the $10,000. This was excellent business judgment and if carried through the market as intelligently as he used it in his business deals he would be a very successful operator.

The wheat market is an immense affair, reaching out into every big country on the globe and yet to operate in wheat futures is a very simple matter. The very simplicity of wheat trading makes it dangerous to the amateur or to the one who is of indolent mind. Its simplicity does not make it safe. Only intelligent study and an iron bound determination not to over-trade will avail. Learn before you earn is a good motto for the trader. The amount of profits which you earn will be in direct ratio to the amount of correct knowledge you acquire about the market, and in the whole range of business there is nothing that will render rewards more lavishly and more rapidly than the wheat market when it is followed according to its basic laws. Every book in this course has something new for the student and the best things are to follow.

COURTS UPHOLD SHORT SELLING AND SPECULATION

Below is an opinion rendered by Justice Holmes of the U. S. Supreme Court in a case of the Board of Trade vs. Christie Grain and Stock Co.

"Of course, in a modern market contracts are not confined to sales for immediate delivery. People will endeavor to forecast the future and to make agreements according to their prophecy. Speculation of this kind by competent men is the self-adjustment of society to the probable. Its value is well known as a means of avoiding or mitigating catastrophes, equalizing prices and providing for periods of want. It is true that the success of the strong induces imitation by the weak and that incompetent persons bring themselves to ruin by undertaking to speculate in their turn. But legislatures and courts generally have recognized that the natural evolutions of a complex society are to be touched only with a very cautious hand and that such coarse attempts at a remedy for the waste incident to every social function as a simple prohibition and laws to stop its being, are harmful and vain. This court has upheld sales of stock for future delivery."

BOOK FOUR

THE POWER OF A NEW IDEA

A new idea is a source of inspiration, unlocking latent powers of the mind. It brings unexpected abilities to the surface and draws a crystal spring of welling enthusiasm up from the subterranean depths of the soul. To the searcher for knowledge a broadening new idea is like a shimmering green valley which bursts on the view of the trudging pioneer as he comes to the crest of a rocky ridge and looks out over a verdant expanse before him. Below is the deep green of the woodland, the flower-sprinkled grass and the winding, life-giving stream that threads its way along emerald banks through fertile meadows. It is a land of promise to the pioneer, just as a new idea becomes a land of promise to the searcher for truth. Witness Marconi as he catches the first glimpse of wireless telegraphy, Stevenson with the steam engine, Whitney with the cotton gin or Edison as he harnessed electricity to work for the people of the world.

The human mind becomes surfeited with old deadening routines and craves new fields. Progress must break the old boundaries as the bird breaks its shell. The human being is a growing, pulsating, eager, ambitious organism constantly storming against the barriers of one era in order that it may march through and into the unexplored era beyond. A fresh idea is a bright new tool, a new road, a welcome talisman, to help the explorer in the development of his chosen new country.

A NEW FEATURE IN MARKET SCIENCE

We now come to a particular type of action found frequently in the grain market and in the actions of New York stocks, in fact, in everything which has price movements, and most of this book will be devoted to expounding this very remarkable style of action. It is manifested in the market where there is a rapid and orderly rise in prices. It does not fit downward action of the market but is found solely in markets that are advancing. A sharp advance causes a "strain" in the market of which, in Book Two, you have already had a brief description. The trader cannot get a clear idea of this movement unless he is keeping a chart of the daily action of stocks or grains in which it occurs but, once it is seen and studied, it will be easily remembered. Prices are the product of thought. If human beings always thought logically and with perfect judgment then the movement about to be described here would never be seen. The changes in the prices of commodities or stocks is an attempt to establish a value that is **thought to be correct**, but which may be far from correct after a little cool reasoning. From this statement you will note the importance of psychology, sometimes referred to as the "psychology of the market" but which is nothing more or less than the wavering efforts of the masses to correctly judge prices.

The whole machinery of the market, including the fluctuating and the recording of values, is born of an intense desire on the part of human beings to make money, to acquire success, to get the needed things of life; and being only human, they over-estimate or over-step. They establish imaginary values which must be corrected by later and more mature thought and by the balancing judgment of wiser heads which help to correct errors after the waves of enthusiasm or of fear have wrought havoc in the market. This sudden straining of the market leads to quick shifts in prices which show up with outstanding clearness on the chart and furnish the trader with an invaluable means of detecting the balancing movement or readjustment which is to follow. The chief value of the movement which the student trader is now to take up, is the fact that it places the market in a **forecastable position**. A very large number of market movements furnish no indication whatever of future action and are, therefore, a total loss to the trader. When decipherable movements are available they should be studied with meticulous care.

3

THE RETURN MOVEMENT

When the trend of the grain market sets powerfully in one direction, as often happens, the price movement usually culminates in fast action. If the price has been traveling upward, this fast action will be in the form of a **vertical rise.** If the price has been traveling downward, the movement will end with a vertical break.

A final, vertical rise nearly always terminates the advance and is followed by a reversal to downtrend. A final, vertical break terminates the downward movement and is followed by a reversal to uptrend.

After a vertical rise at the top of a bull market the trend turns down very quickly but after a vertical break, ending a bear market, the trend may be slow in turning upward because the bullish element amongst traders is discouraged and quits the market for awhile. At the top of bull movements, people are in high spirits. Profit taking and short selling develop on a large scale and cause big swings and finally a finishing break.

While a vertical rise terminates a bull market, yet there are many big swings throughout the market movement which show the application of this new principle which you are now learning and which is termed the "Return Movement." It always follows a vertical rise or a vertical break. Often a return movement develops into a combined affair as shown from July 25 to August 11 on the oats chart, page 7. At the beginning of the study of this remarkable movement the student should first understand how to determine the trend of the market and for this purpose KEY NUMBER THREE should be applied. While the return movement works in either kind of a market—bull or bear—yet the trader, to make successful deals, acquires best success by first establishing the trend. Vertical rises and vertical breaks are all the way from a small range of two or three cents to a big range of ten to fifteen cents. Yet in each case the action is the same. The market returns to practically the point from which it started, as will be noted on the chart to follow. Some little skill is necessary to determine where the market is turning and we might suggest that the minor trend line, shown in Book three, is your best help for detecting the turns when they are at the tops of swings.

4

A slowly climbing market, such as that shown on the oats chart from March 23 to May 27, has frequent reactions that neutralize each other. Traders even up their accounts mostly but buying for "the long pull" predominates and the price advances until it begins to incubate bullish opinion. Then, at last, there is the general scramble to buy grain and the vertical rise, finishing the movement, occurs as you see it in the chart from May 27 to May 31.

In the preceding paragraph you have the life history of most bull movements in wheat or other grains. When the vertical rise comes the temptation to sell out long grain becomes dominant. A few new buyers, "eleventh hour bulls," enter the market around top figures, who absorb the profit taking sales and for awhile hold the market. Three days of narrow action are noted at the top of the oats chart. At last, short sellers and profit takers predominate and the decline begins.

The decline from May 31 to June 27 is the RETURN MOVEMENT. It is considered finished when it retraces the ground covered by the vertical rise, therefore, the return movement is based upon a very positive axiom as follows:

FUNDAMENTAL AXIOM

> In the market movement of stocks and of grain options the price always passes over the ground twice.

If the price advances with an approximate vertical upward movement it will, at last, halt and either gradually or rapidly travel **down again,** passing over the ground covered by the vertical rise.

If the price breaks with an approximate vertical downward movement it will, at last, halt and either gradually or rapidly travel **upward again,** passing over the ground covered by the vertical break.

In these two last paragraphs you have the simplified history of the "return movement." It now devolves upon the student to apply it to a variety of different market years and the numerous movements that occur in grains during these years.

5

VERTICAL MOVEMENTS

Since vertical movements figure so largely in the application of the return movement it is necessary to enlarge upon these at this time. Vertical movements of considerable extent occur frequently at intermediate stages of either a bull or bear market. Often a sharp swing begins with a vertical movement and is sometimes called a "standing jump." Such a straight-up advance invariably limits the extent of the swing as it places the market in an **over-bought** condition. Profit taking and short selling by a host of small traders take place on such advances and cause their termination.

A large number of these intermediate or small vertical movements occurred during the long decline in the stock market from the high top of 1929 down to the bottom in July, 1932. These appeared both as vertical declines and vertical advances. Examples will be given of each type in the succeeding pages of this book.

The return movement is considered as one of the fundamentals of market action because it appears in the price movement of all commodities in which the public speculates or trades. However, for our purpose, we may employ the grains as the chief means of illustrating this interesting and very profitable move.

A multiplicity of rules for market procedure may be interesting but they are extremely confusing. The difficulty with minor rules is that they too often fail. The only sure success in the speculative market comes from a knowledge of the few powerful, basic laws, or phenomena that motivate the market. Long observation and market experience have taught the writer the futility of depending upon small schemes, artifices, market tricks, stop loss orders, key days and other vague means by which small traders attempt to snatch a meager profit from the market. Speculation involves the high risk based upon the probability of receiving a high profit and the reason so many fail is because they use minor tools to accomplish a big task. Too many people scorn market knowledge when they should be making a profound study of it.

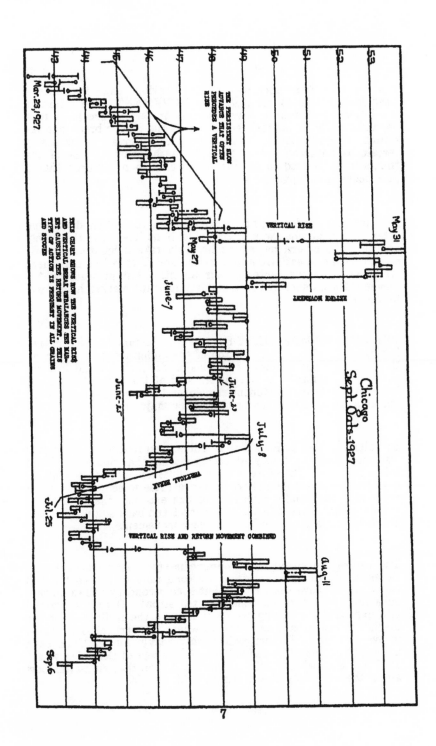

Chicago
Sept. Oats -1927

The chart of September oats on the previous page furnishes a clear introduction to the RETURN MOVEMENT. The return is the action which follows a vertical rise or vertical break. It may be, and usually is, impossible to forecast the rise or break but the return after the rise or break is practically certain or as nearly certain as anything ever gets to be in the market. One of the things most desired in market practice is to be assured that a good move is coming.

The amateur trader might not know from the action developing after March 23 what was to come but if he knew one thing only and that the return movement he could take a handsome profit on the decline in oats from May 31 to June 7. It is this movement which is to be the center of our attention but in studying the movement a number of other highly important market habits will be disclosed.

THE RETURN MOVEMENT has a very important function in that it practically always calls the top of the major trend of a market. It often calls the bottom of the major downward trend but not with such regularity as it calls the end of the upward trend. It is important that the student remember that the grain and stock markets are always in major uptrend or major downtrend.

By referring back to Book Two it will be seen that many big moves were preceded by a slowly advancing market that finally developed into a fast rise. Therefore, a long, gradual advance often—though not always—forecasts a sharp or vertical rise to come. The "trading mind" continually runs first to one extreme, then the other, from the bear market to the bull market and back again. The oats chart depicts a complete bull and bear movement.

The return movement sets in immediately after a vertical rise. Occasionally, though not often, a second rally or second top will carry prices above the first top but such secondary rallies quickly subside. The return movement is too strong. Once the vertical rise exhausts the buying power of a move the inclination of the market to break back or return to where the vertical rise started is overpowering. Further rallies meet heavy selling. Turn back to page 33 of Book Two and note the double tops of December wheat 1929 and May wheat 1927. In these it is seen that no matter how sharp the secondary rise it cannot hold.

8

By a study of KEY NUMBER TWO in Book Four the student will see that the lower closing of May 31 in the oats chart, gives the first signal that the top is made, that the vertical rise is ended and that the return movement is in possession of the market. Naturally, the next question the student would ask is:

HOW FAR DOWN WILL THE RETURN MOVEMENT EXTEND?

We must limit the extent of the movement to the FUNDAMENTAL AXIOM stated on page 5. The return normally travels back over the distance covered by the vertical rise or the vertical break. The final decline may carry prices far beyond such limits but variations to this are unimportant. The chief consideration now is to follow this return movement through the various large and small movements of the different grains and, also, study the way it operates in stocks or other commodities.

In the oats chart on Page 7 it is evident that the break or return from the top on May 31 should be down to 47½, this being the level from which the vertical rise started. This is accomplished on June 7 and a little over. Sometimes the return will overrun and at other times will fall somewhat short. Price movements do not run with mathematical accuracy though often they are approximately accurate. The wise trader would accept profits on a short sale (made around the top or anywhere down the line) at least one cent before the return movement was completed. While the return was due to drop back to 47½ he would make sure by taking profits at 48½.

It is notable that on June 23 the market started breaking but halted on June 25. This vertical break was quickly recovered by the return movement. But since the return movement shows many extra large "returns" the trader should wait for the best ones rather than attempt to catch the smaller movements. Small movements end quickly before the trader expects them to, while the large return movements afford ample time to think and make plans.

Starting about July 11 oats began a liquidation movement which continued rather steadily downward to July 25. There was no rally of as much as one cent in the six cent break, although the decline covered some thirteen days. This decline—July 11 to July 25—amounts to a vertical break.

It would have been impossible for the novice to foresee the break but with a knowledge of the return movement the student would have known a recovery in price was due and that the recovery would retrace the ground covered on the break. The thirteen-day congestion before and after July 25 is a signal to the market student that "accumulation" is quietly taking place by professionals and that this accumulation will be followed by a rise. It should be understood that there are many clever operators who are aware of these movements and who have become wealthy following them. A break like the one we are discussing tells them plainly that it will be easy to push prices upward after the break.

It is not professionals alone who cause a rise after a break. Others buy for an expected rise, simply on the old rule of "buy on a break." The sum total of this buying results in the rise such as you see from July 25 to August 11. This rise constitutes the **return movement**. It, also, amounts to a vertical rise and is, therefore, subject to a decline. That is why it becomes a **combined** vertical rise and return movement.

The student will naturally ask why the break from May 31 to June was not a vertical break that should be followed by a rise or return movement. The answer is that this was a completed bull movement in oats in which the rise from May 27 to May 31 was neutralized by the break back to June 7. A completed top need not have a return movement, although many tops have several rapid breaks and rallies.

The vertical rise and return movement combined, as shown from July 25 to August 11, was not a bull movement. It was a manipulated affair. The real bull move had taken place and was over. Doubtless, the same people who bought for the rally to August 11 sold short around top figures knowing that an equal break was to come. By September 6 the oats price was back down to the starting place of March 23. This decline, also, constituted a return movement.

THE PERSISTENT RETURN MOVEMENT

Perhaps not more than 1% of the total number of people trading in grain keep a chart of its actions. Only a comparatively few remember the recent highs and lows and therefore, have only a faint understanding of the successive steps by which the market moves into downtrend and uptrend. The great readjusting trends of the wheat market, by which it moves slowly from heavy overproduction to decisive underproduction, are stately and impressive. Few understand them because they do not take the time to chart such movements or to study them. The bull and bear movements are but incidents in these big trends. Then, dropping down to the lesser movements, these **return movements** are but incidents in the bull and bear movements.

Individual traders are deeply interested in these smaller movements because they see them in operation and are either consciously or unconsciously using them. The return movement, while but a small incident in a big economic trend of wheat, is nevertheless powerful and so persistent that it can be used for excellent profit. Very few traders have the patience or inclination to play for long pull although the largest profits are made in the long pull movements. So many buy and sell for short turns that it is necessary to understand the smaller movements and no type of action is more important than the return movement. The wheat market is always in uptrend or downtrend. It never stops until either a bull market is completed or a bear market is completed. These vertical rises, vertical breaks and the **return** are incidental movements in the major trends.

As far as possible it is well for the student trader to remove himself from those who are affected by statistics such as the visible supply, export business, monthly crop reports, and Liverpool quotations. These are of secondary importance and whatever effect they may have appears in the chart action of wheat. It is desirable that one keep posted on the progress of crops, carry-over and weather but depend on chart movements to furnish indications for the future.

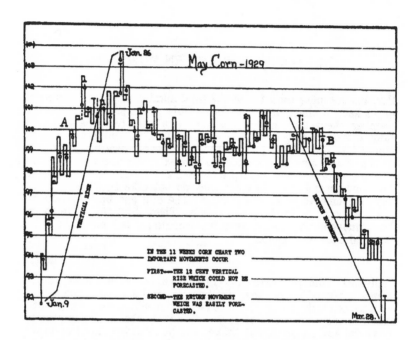

Chart labels: Jan. 26 · May Corn -1929 · A · B · VERTICAL RISE · VERTICAL MOVEMENT · Jan. 9 · Mar. 28.

IN THE 11 WEEKS CORN CHART TWO
IMPORTANT MOVEMENTS OCCUR

FIRST——THE 12 CENT VERTICAL
RISE WHICH COULD NOT BE
FORECASTED.

SECOND——THE RETURN MOVEMENT
WHICH WAS EASILY FORE-
CASTED.

TWO MONTHS IN MAKING TOP

While corn displays less activity than wheat it is reasonably active
at high levels. In the chart above it will be noted that the vertical
rise, from January 9 to January 26, was completed in sixteen days
but that the price hovered around top levels for nearly fifty days
before the always persistent return movement finally brought it
down to the level from which it started. The student trader, in
charting corn, would at once have been attracted to this powerful
advance beginning January 9 and would have watched for top action. The first break from 102½ gives the signal that the move
is ending. From then on, until the price is back down to 92, this
option is a sale on any rally on a two-cent scale up. In this case
many profits might have been taken, but the easiest and largest
profits would have been made by selling around 102 or above and
holding for the break at 91 as it was evident from the first that the
price would eventually drop back there. After a vertical rise, that
results in a high top for a grain like the above, it is seldom the price
return movement.

12

VERTICAL BREAK AND RETURN MOVEMENT IN THE POUND STERLING.

In September, 1931, England went off the gold standard, causing a sharp break in the quoted value of the pound sterling.

In financial circles the currency of other nations is bought and sold much as commodities are traded in in the American grain market. Anything, having a speculative or s h i f t i n g v a l u e, follows approximately the same general market action as the one constant and unchangeable factor is human nature.

In the chart of Sterling — here shown — the student will note the sharp break from Oct. 21 to the final bottom, Dec. 8. This is a vertical break. It was caused by financial difficulties in Great Britain which for awhile increased after that country went off the gold standard. French bankers and many others sold sterling short expecting to buy it cheaper. With the recovery of English finances there was a rush to buy sterling and the usual return movement occurred as shown.

By April 15, sterling had recovered 83% of the vertical break. Thus, in a very unusual commodity, the return movement is found to run true to form.

Other commodities—sugar, lard, cotton, coffee, eggs, butter, etc. —are fully as susceptible to this movement.

13

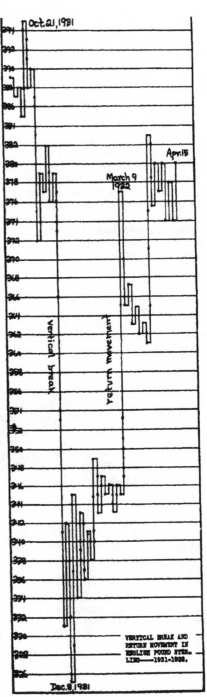

SHARP MOVEMENTS ARE IMPORTANT

In the first place they are clear. They stand out on the chart as distinct and different from the usual small meandering movements but the most important deduction to be made is that sharp action, such as the vertical rise and the **return movement**, disturb the equilibrium of the market. It marks the culmination of one trend and inaugurates another. Slow movements may give little evidence of the future action of an option but a sharp break or vertical rise is an **immediate signal** that a change of trend is near. It may be a permanent change or a temporary change of trend but, at least, it is important.

A vertical break of considerable extent is known, amongst professional traders, as furnishing a good place to buy a grain. A goodly rally is practically assured. Also short sellers, who have thus been given a profit, buy in their lots and join the buying crowd. Then the market advances.

By the same tokens a vertical rise brings into the market a wave of profit taking and short selling—and the market declines. The attempt to follow the short, daily movements is a serious mistake. Occasionally wealthy speculators take a hand in these small "in and out" trades but eventual loss is certain if anyone tries to follow the daily movements. Pit traders, who have no commissions to pay, may make money but the "local" trader should try for the big movements only.

It has long been the dream of amateur market students to discover some mechanical means that would sit astride the daily movements and grind out profits but such schemes are doomed to failure. There is no getting around the fact that the most important requirement, in either stocks or grains, is accurate forecasts. The successful business man becomes so because of his ability to foresee the outcome of his merchandising plans or of whatever business he is exploiting. Stock analyses furnish useful information but they are useless as forecasts.

14

PROTRACTED MOVEMENTS

Extensive movements often occur in the grains with the price traveling in one direction for several months. Such movements usually proceed by stages. There are halting periods as shown at A, B, C and D on the wheat chart, page 16. The price tries repeatedly to recover but the pressure is too heavy and it continues on down until, as in this case, liquidation is complete. Then comes the recovery. A halting stage in a downward movement is not always a sign that the price is recovering or preparing to make its return movement. When the price broke ten cents below that of June 29 the student trader would have been justified in buying wheat at 56 on the expectation of a recovery by the return movement, but he would have had to carry his grain down to 45—11 points lower—before the return began in earnest. If he is trading by correct principles, as will be shown in later books in this course, he will be buying more wheat on a scale down and would own wheat at any stage on down to 45. His safeguard is in the knowledge that the price will eventually return and render him his profit, but he must margin and hold his lots through or he will lose.

THESE LONG RANGE DECLINES may often be forecasted, though not always. The author, in a long range forecast issued to clients in November, 1930, forecasted the ultimate low for wheat as 48 to 52 to be reached by the end of July, 1931. The actual bottom was reached at 44⅝ on October 5, 1931. These long range forecasts are not difficult as will be shown further on and the most difficult part for the student will be to believe what the chart tells him. Turning again to the chart on page 16, it is seen that a vertical break may be a prolonged affair. This has been noted in previous charts herein but the very extensive vertical break from June 29 to September 21 serves a good purpose here by convincing the student that, regardless of the extent of a vertical rise or vertical break, the return movement is none the less certain. By referring to Book Two, pages 17 and 18, the reader will see an advance which covered a period of six months followed by a complete return movement retracing the entire extent of the advance. The return was completed in a little more than sixty days. It is thus seen that a powerful movement in one direction is balanced by a powerful movement in the opposite direction.

15

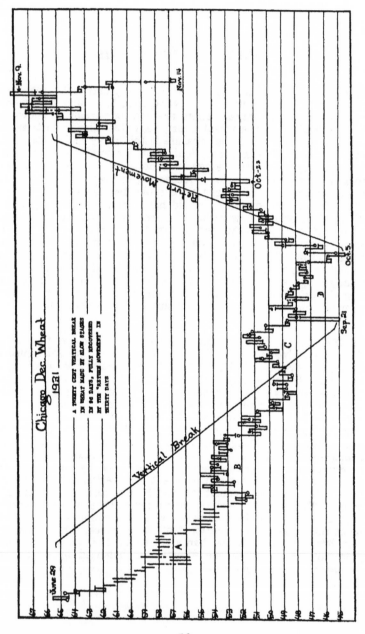

Chicago Dec. Wheat
1931

A VERY CLEAN VERTICAL BREAK
IN WHEAT MADE BY SLOW STAGES
IN 86 DAYS, FULLY RECOVERED
BY THE "RETURN MOVEMENT" IN
THIRTY DAYS

Vertical Break

Return Movement

June 29

Sep. 21

Oct. 5

Oct. 23

Nov. 14

Nov. 9

A

B

C

D

16

WHAT CAUSED THE RETURN MOVEMENT as shown from
October 5 to November 9 on page 16?

First —The extreme low price, lowest known in wheat
history.
Second—The elimination of weakly margined accounts.
Third —An increasing number of speculators expecting
higher prices and wishing to participate in them.

It is always to be remembered by the student that a goodly number
of experienced speculators are aware of the effect of these vertical
movements upon the market. They are watching for them. They
keep careful charts with a view to catching the market in a vulnerable position and when a situation develops, such as shown in
the break of wheat to the 45 level, they are ready to enter the
market with buying orders. One speculator reasons that wheat,
having at last reached new lows for all time, will naturally develop
a smart rally. Another speculator discovers, from confidential con-
nections with brokers, that the "weak holders" of wheat have been
forced out and reasons that the next movement will naturally be
upward. Then enters the public speculator **en masse**, a constantly
increasing group, which has been waiting for something like a rise
to show a new trend. On the advance, that takes place from October
5 and upward, the "public" begins to buy heavily and to **pyramid**
by buying more on the way up. Thus the combined result of all of
this buying power is to force a strong advance developing into a
bull movement as this is.

The rise from October 5 to the top is not only the **return movement** but also a **bull movement.** In our Daily Service to clients the
complete advance was forecasted from October 5 to November 9 and
is a matter of record.

The student will naturally wish to know how we forecasted this top
but again we must defer the answer until the last book of the
course where some of the most important things are concentrated.
The student quickly discovers that the bull move, here shown, is
also developing a **vertical rise** on the way up from October 23 to
the top and will correctly reason out the fact that a return from
the top down to the October 23 level will ensue. This break was
fully consummated before the end of November.

17

SMALL TRADERS AND SMALL MOVEMENTS

The multitude of small movements occurring and the restless action through each trading day are the product of a vast army of traders dealing in small lots of from one to twenty thousand bushels. Every exchange has its "locals" who haunt the brokerage house, trading in and out on anything from a half cent to a two cent movement. At the end of the week a large number "evens up" rather than take chances on what Monday might bring forth.

Pit traders, in Chicago and other trading centers such as Minneapolis and Kansas City, often trade rapidly and heavily throughout the day, causing frequent fluctuations not at all based upon crop conditions or upon the demand. These "scalping" operations are, however, a very important part of market action.

The next important group of traders deals in larger lots of wheat but is inclined to wait for sharp swings. It is this class which is responsible for most of the vertical rises and the vertical breaks in market action and the return movements that follow them. They are not interested in small profits, choosing rather to play for eight, ten or even fifteen cent profits and when successful, they are content to wait until conditions seem to justify entering the market again.

Frequently the large traders will buy several hundred thousand bushels of wheat, picking it up on the small reactions at the bottom of a vertical rise in lots of twenty to fifty thousand. A ten cent advance with a lot of 500,000, yields the very desirable sum of $50,000 from which the trader can well allow the commission of $1,250.

A third class of traders, very small in number, but perhaps the best informed and most daring of all operators, is interested cnly in the big bull and bear markets. They will wait a year or more in quiet seclusion for the proper time. When they believe the time right they accumulate **millions of bushels** to start with and add to their lines when the move gets under way. They get "interviews" in the papers and bull news in the associated press and, when the public rushes enthusiastically into the market, they sell out and often SELL SHORT!

18

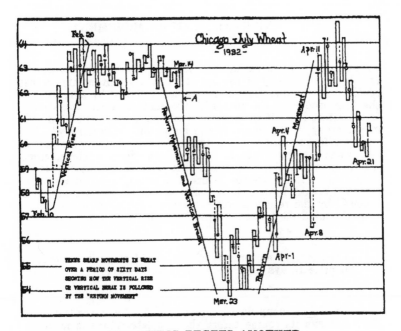

ONE SWING BEGETS ANOTHER

Beginning with the wheat market on February 10, in the above chart, the student trader could not have readily known of the sharp advance which was to carry the price up to 64, but once the movement was accomplished, he would have been aware that a "strain" was developing which would pull prices down again. The rise was "vertical." The three weeks of dull movements around 63 show clearly that the advance has been arrested. Any considerable pause in the market after a vertical rise is practically sure to be followed by a return down to the starting place. The reason for this is that traders become discouraged when the market does not proceed on upward and sell out. This selling stops the advance and starts the break.

When the price dropped below the point A, or below the top congestion level, it amounted to a confirmation of the **return movement** to the starting level of February 10.

But unexpected weakness carried prices down to 54. Again the student had no means of forecasting the full extent of the break but, since it amounted to a **vertical break** as shown on the chart, he could be positive of a sharp rally or, in other words, the "return movement" to around 63 where the break originated.

19

LARGE AND SMALL RETURN MOVEMENTS

So persistent is the market in making these return movements that a large majority of the one and two day movements, if they continue in one direction that long, are followed by a return. In the first studies of the author on the subject, a rule was devised to the effect that "if the price of wheat rises above the high point of yesterday it will return to the high point of yesterday." This was an effort to furnish a way to use the small or daily movements but it was confusing because the price sometimes continued climbing for many days and it seemed that the rule was wrong. It has been found more accurate to use the terms "vertical rise" and "vertical break" in describing the type of movements that will be followed by the return movement and for the sake of impressing it on the mind the fundamental axiom is here repeated:

In the market movements of stocks and of grain options the price always passes over the ground twice.

It is sometimes many days or even weeks after a vertical movement has run its course before the complete return is made and these longer times are the most profitable because the trader can espouse one side and stay faithful to that side until the final return is made. A very excellent example of a long detained return is found in the chart on pages 20-21 of September wheat for 1927. In this case the vertical rise began April 9, finished the advance by May 31 but did not get back down to the starting point until the following September.

The extraordinary value of the return movement is illustrated by the chart on pages 20-21 as it becomes at once clear that any short sale, made after the top signal was given, would have yielded a sure profit. Also any line of short sales on a scale up on any of the May rallies would have yielded a handsome profit.

The student cannot impress this movement too deeply upon his mind as it is one of the very best things in all market action. Several lesser vertical movements are noticeable on the chart on page 19 as, for instance, the one from April 1 to April 4, an advance of about five points with most of the return made by April 8. The student may inspect every movement in this chart and he will find that the inclination to return—to pass a second time over the ground—is one of the strong features of market action.

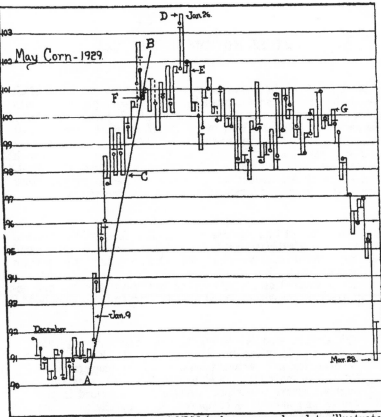

THE ABOVE CHART OF CORN is here reproduced to illustrate the unerring action of the **return incentive** in the market. This chart was primarily intended to show the use of the minor trend line and was used in Book Three, page 11. The student may now see how two powerful market habits work hand in hand with each other and for the direct benefit of the trader if he will but use them.

The minor trend line A - - B tells where the market is turning downward. The return movement tells how far down the price will go.

An uninformed trader would be utterly confused by the long series of desultory movements from F. to G. He would be constantly imbued with a belief that the market was about to proceed on upward. He would thus be wrong and would lose. Our student reader, knowing that the price was already at a heavy strain to react, would take the short side and stay for the final break to the level reached March 28.

21

RETURN MOVEMENT IN STOCKS

So powerful is this important movement in the market action of all speculative issues and commodities that an example is herewith given of the way the movement occurs in U. S. Steel. It appears frequently throughout the movements of all stocks but is most frequent and extensive in active issues. While it is very common in U. S. Steel, as shown by the chart on page 23, it is found with greater frequency and is of greater extent in American Can, Eastman Kodak or Air Reduction. The lower priced a grain or stock becomes the fewer and smaller the return movements that occur.

The importance of this movement is that it is **forecastable.** Vertical breaks and vertical rises are as extensive and are often more rapid but they come without warning. To catch them and trade on them is sheer accident. But when they have happened the trader is practically assured of the return and can, with calmness and decision, trade on the correct trend until the movement is completed.

The student who is trading actively and studying this course should, when he finds the market developing a vertical rise or a vertical break, study the phenomena of the return movement, as shown in this book, very thoroughly. Every important movement is described in the course and should be compared with the charts in the course that fit them. Compare the charts you are making with those in these books and you will find it possible to forecast some very wonderful moves.

One of the reasons why many traders fail on the market is because they become centered upon the small daily movements which are constantly dancing like the small waves on the ocean. These little ripples are impossible to forecast. But the TIDES CAN BE FORECASTED. When the tide comes in the man on the shore knows that at the proper time it will go out. And likewise when it is out he knows it will perform a "return movement" and come in again. One of the secrets of success is in trading upon the big, known movements of the market.

U. S. Steel, in declining from the high top of 261¾, reached in the

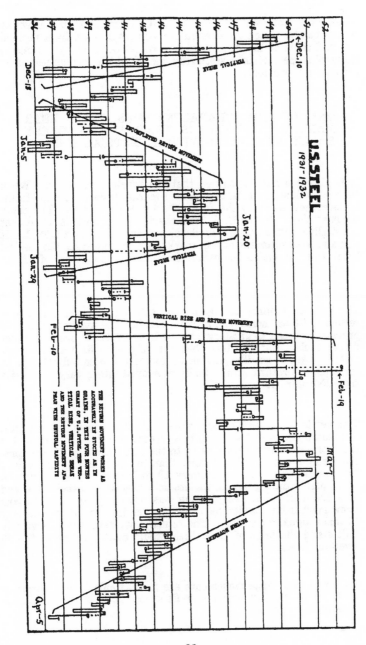

U.S. STEEL
1931-1932

23

fall of 1929, underwent seven extensive rallies on its way down to 30 and below. Each of these rallies was emphasized by a vertical rise and some of the more extensive rallies contained from one to three of these vertical rises, every one of which was succeeded by the return movement.

ONE OF THE CHARACTERISTICS OF A BEAR MARKET IN STOCKS IS THAT ALMOST EVERY RALLY IS INITIATED WITH A VERTICAL RISE.

It is almost a sure indication that the break is not over. When the real bull move starts, after a bear market is completed in stocks, it never gets away in the form of a big vertical rise. The climb becomes slow. In the U. S. Steel chart on page 23 it is noted that the decline halted and a rally developed on December 18, 1931. It was an endeavor on the part of market action, to retrace the vertical break from December 10 down to December 18, a distance of fifteen points.

The rally to January 20 was a good attempt to make the rise or return to 51 but some sort of news assailed the market, causing a premature break to January 29. This last vertical break was not forecastable. But the fact that the return to 51 was not completed makes it readily possible to forecast a renewed attempt to complete the return which finally developed into a very sharp rise from February 10.

The vertical rise and return movement shown was forecastable. The author knows of at least, two forecast services that predicted the entire rise from February 10 to the top, February 19, the forecast being made on nothing other than the certainty of the return. The sprawling top from February 19 to March 7 was the distributing period during which traders sold long U. S. Steel stock and took the short side. Liquidation was not complete. Those who knew market laws understood that the vertical rise after February 10 was a signal for selling. The return movement would inevitably follow and the price of U. S. Steel would again decline to the 36 level—or lower.

Thus two very large movements are forecastable in this period of U. S. Steel, the advance above February 10 and the full break back to 36.

WHAT'S FIRST IN IMPORTANCE?

Correct trend is the first thing to be determined. Without knowledge of the major trend of a market the speculator is sailing an unknown sea. The student trader should constantly impress upon his mind the necessity of detecting the long range destination of the grain in which he is preparing to trade. You have been learning of two kinds of trend, the Major trend and Minor trend. Another form of trend has been operating in a hidden manner in the world wheat market, and that is the ECONOMIC TREND.

Economic trends run for a series of years. They represent the length of time it takes to run from crushing overproduction back to serious underproduction. For the trader's use it is highly interesting and a part of the cultural education of a well posted student of the wheat market. Some attempt has been made by market observers to resolve these economic trends into seven year cycles. The author of this course finds no such time limit to them. Our largest U. S. crop of wheat was raised in 1915, 1,025,801,000 bushels. From this heavy production we ran (through the great war) to 1925, during which year our crop was 676,479,000 bushels, thus requiring **ten years** to run from overproduction to underproduction.

The next cycle started with the short crop of 1925 and continued to 1931, a period of **six years**. The cause of the rapid, heavy production of wheat was the great increase of tractors on farms and the invention of the combine. A small number of farmers could handle a vast amount of wheat acreage and easily grew more wheat than could be consumed. Thus we had the six years **economic downtrend** which ended in October, 1931.

WHAT NEXT? Naturally, wheat will be in uptrend for years to come, five—seven—ten years. No one can tell. The low prices of 1931 and early 1932 will give way to extravagantly high prices in the years to come. This uptrend will be interspersed with many bull and bear movements, each one rising higher than the previous one until another grand climax of prices occurs like those during the war period.

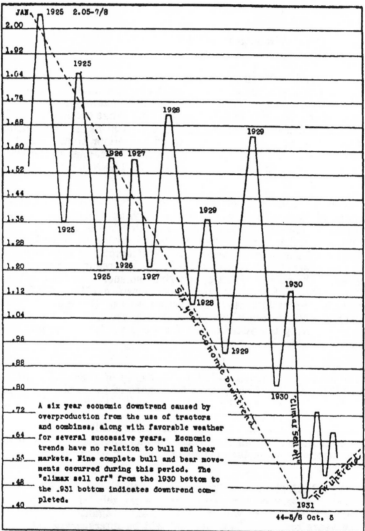

JAN. 1925 2.05-7/8

A six year economic downtrend caused by overproduction from the use of tractors and combines, along with favorable weather for several successive years. Economic trends have no relation to bull and bear markets. Nine complete bull and bear movements occurred during this period. The "climax sell off" from the 1930 bottom to the .931 bottom indicates downtrend completed.

44-5/8 Oct. 5

The above chart of the recent six year economic downtrend from 1925-1932 is a clear picture of the way prices will adjust themselves to the law of supply and demand. Canada, Argentine, Russia, Australia and the United States, all heavy exporting countries, began overproducing wheat following the high price of 1925 which made wheat growing immensely profitable. A steel plant or motor factory can cut production at a month's notice, but it takes years to force agriculture out of a favorite crop. The six year decline finally drove many wheat growers out of production through sheer insolvency. But Nature also proves an effective agent in checking economic declines by cutting crops heavily in various parts of the world.

THE POWERFUL ECONOMIC TREND

Students, accustomed to studying major trends and minor trends in the ordinary sense of the word, should not confuse these with the economic trend which is an entirely separate thing. Starting down from the high level of 1925 it will be observed that nine bull and bear markets have occurred. Some of them were very large. The rise, during 1924 to the top reached in January, 1925, covered seven months. Some of the bull markets did not extend more than twenty-five to thirty cents, but in every case the price of wheat dropped down from the bull market tops to make still lower prices.

During an economic downtrend of prices the successive bear markets drop to new lows until the decline has been completed.

During an economic uptrend of prices each successive bear market fails to drop as low as the one previous.

During the latter half of 1925 and also during 1928 and 1929, there were some extra big bull movements. They were brought on by a heavy speculative demand which is never permanent. The demand for food is permanent but the demand for wheat, as a speculative investment, vanishes when the speculator takes his profit. Small crop shortages, such as occurred in 1927 and in 1929 when the Canadian crop was short, did not sufficiently reduce the heavy world overproduction. Therefore, the economic trend declined until more wheat acreage was put out of business.

A striking example of an unhealthy advance occurred when wheat reached bottom at 93½ (May option) in 1929. In early June, 1929, it was reported in big headlines in a Chicago paper that the farm board, newly appointed, had been tendered $100,000,000 to use in the wheat market. This gave the speculators the chance they wanted. Canada was already suffering somewhat from dry weather, which fact, along with the sensational farm board news, sent wheat upward for a sixty cent advance. As a matter of fact the farm board had not received any money at all and the Canadian crop for that year was 304,000,000 bushels.

The final drop from the high top of 1929 to the bottom of 1932 was inevitable.

CAN ECONOMIC TRENDS BE FORECASTED

It is more difficult to forecast economic trends because there are no sharp keys of market action to indicate the turns. The sole cause of economic uptrend is underproduction. Overproduction is the cause of downtrend. Years are required to pile up a surplus too heavy to market. Often Nature steps in with several short crops and temporarily balances an accumulating surplus. That postpones the decline. A clear example of this is shown in 1925-1926-1927 where wheat held for three years near the $1.20 line before resuming downtrend.

The change to economic uptrend usually occurs through a wheat crop disaster. The 1931-1932 wheat crop met disaster from the start of the sowing season. Dry weather at seeding time and wireworms that consumed the seed as fast as sown, beset the crop. That part of the western crop which came up met further drought in the spring. Dust storms destroyed large areas. In March a bitter freeze did heavy damage to the crop both east and west. In May, 1932 the Department of Agriculture estimated a reduction under the previous year of 346,000,000 bushels of winter wheat. Russia, in 1931, harvested little more than a half crop. In all wheat countries insolvency of wheat growers caused a heavy loss of acreage. Thus the tide of overproduction was changed and the drift towards underproduction began, BUT THIS PROCESS REQUIRED AN ENTIRE CROP YEAR.

Starting from the bottom level of 44⅝, reached October 5, 1931, the economic uptrend began as shown by the dotted line and appears definite.

HOW DO WE KNOW the trend has turned definitely upward? That's the natural question every student will ask. Frankly, I must say there is no absolutely certain way to prove it but I find circumstantial evidence strong enough to satisfy us. First, the stock market was down to the zone in the Dow-Jones Industrials between 42-65 where, for thirty-two years, every bear market ended. Second, the price of wheat was the lowest ever known in this country and far below the cost of production. Third, the "climax sell off" occurred which usually completes a downtrend. (See chart.) In England the price of wheat in October, 1931 was the lowest in two hundred and fifty years.

Weather is as much responsible for economic trends as the inventions of men and, since weather has no regular cycles of good and bad crop weather, there is no foundation for the idea for seven year cycles of trend.

28

USING THE ECONOMIC TREND

The sole aim of the student is to turn his market knowledge into profits. The thrill one gets from uncovering secrets of market action is that new doors of financial opportunity are opened. The use of the economic trend is highly valuable in planning an extensive campaign of trading. As economic uptrends proceed, each successive bear market will end at a higher level. That is, the only way the price can climb higher over a period of years. Bull market tops in uptrend will be irregular, but occasionally very high tops will be made.

The uptrend is the most suitable to the trading public because 90% are inclined to follow the bull side. Each bull or bear movement can be forecasted and followed by the methods taught in this course with the added advantage that the trader knows **each bear market, during an economic uptrend, will end higher** than the previous one. On pages 26 and 33 of Book III of this course is found a means of using the market in an intensive manner by the "Multi-Profit" trading plan. It will be of vast advantage to know that an economic uptrend is in progress because a buying campaign at the bottom of a bear market becomes doubly sure of success.

ACTIVE TRADING is not retarded by the economic trend, but is greatly facilitated. It gives the operator a deeper knowledge of his subject than is found in market news. He becomes more confident of his position. He ignores the surface news and "financial comments" and goes about his trading, knowing that in following the pronounced and important laws of the market, he can win where others fail.

Several examples might be given the student of economic uptrends and downtrends that have occurred during the last fifty years, but they are similar to the one charted on page 26. It may be said briefly that a twelve year economic **downtrend** started in 1881 and lasted until 1894 following the introduction of the self-binding harvester which vastly reduced the cost of growing wheat. Again, from 1894 to 1917, a long economic **uptrend** prevailed, starting with the Spanish-American war and running almost steadily upward—though slowly—to a culmination in the great world war which sent the price of wheat above $3.00 per bushel.

DETECTING BOTTOMS AND TOPS OF ECONOMIC TRENDS

This is by no means an easy task and fortunately, for the trader, it is not very important. Sometimes it takes two or three years to end an economic downtrend because of the half paralyzed state of industry that prevails at the bottom of depressions.

Perhaps the easiest way to tell when one of these discouraging downtrends is about to end is from the intensity of depression news. When the newspapers print stories of possible revolution and financial disaster and when bodies of men "march" on Washington demanding assistance, depressions are getting to the acute or final stage. It will be remembered that Coxey's Army marched across the country to Washington in 1894, which was the end of a depression (note preceeding page) and at the same time an end to an economic downtrend. Again in 1932, right at the present time, a group of men, purporting to be of the American Legion, originated in the middle west and tramped to Washington where they encamped and demanded assistance from the Government. These tramping mobs do not develop with every small depression, but seem to grow out of extremely bitter depressions such as that of 1894 and the present one of 1932.

Other indications of economic bottoms are free silver harangues, heavy unemployment, extremely dull business and probably the most apparent of all indications is the stock market down to extreme low levels with leading stocks selling at one dollar to ten dollars per share. The tops of economic trends end more quickly. Most of them in past history have reached their tops with the culmination of a war. Our highest one recently occurred during the 1917-1918 period with the ending of the great war.

A knowledge of these economic trends is interesting and cultural, but is not at all necessary to the success of the speculator. However, a knowledge of them teaches the speculator not to become "married" to uptrend or downtrend. The fallacy of this is easily seen in the famous statement of John Pierpont Morgan's "Don't sell America short," which slogan was used entirely to the top of the 1929 bull market. In fact, the only ones who made money after that were those who did "sell America short."

The trading habits of professional operators are far from being as systematic as their success would indicate. Those, whose success has made them national figures, play only for the bull and bear movements. Their trading, during the six year economic downtrend charted on page 26, found two of these really brilliant men completely deceived by the trend. Twice they mistook temporary rallies for the beginning of uptrend and were forced to sell out at a loss.

Some big operators work best on the bull side. Mr. Arthur Cutten seems to have achieved his largest success by operations on the long side. Mr. Jesse Livermore is sometimes referred to as the "World's Greatest Bear." While he is said to operate on either the upside or downside, his outstanding achievements have been on the short side.

When the professional believes he sees conditions in the wheat crop that justify a bull move he begins to "feel out the market." He buys in frequent, moderate sized lots through several brokers to see whether a systematic program of buying will lift the market. If the market absorbs the buying without advancing materially, the buying is stopped and perhaps all the grain thus acquired, sold out. It naturally causes a loss but the loss of ten or twenty thousand dollars is of little consequence to a trader who is planning a "coup" that will return a million.

When the market advances satisfactorily the professional refrains from buying until a reaction develops, then he enters the market again to turn it upward with a number of rapidly executed trades. His plan is to stop the breaks and at the same time to increase his line. The public, always delighted to get into a bull move, comes to his assistance. The advance is carried up and up. Sometimes the professional, having accumulated a line of millions, decides to lighten his load on some particularly strong day. This naturally causes a reaction and while the break is on, he repurchases lower than he sold out, thus renewing his line. This was done several times by the largest operators in the bull move of 1926. Records are available to prove this.

Following a sharp, high topped bull move, the downward swings are large and violent.

Such activity affords an excellent opportunity for the skilled professional. He loves action. He has other lesser but still powerful traders working with him to keep up the action. Our readers have already learned that the downward movements, after a sharp top, are in the form of long, active swings and sharp rebounds. This is the result of trading on a huge scale by professionals. The chart on page 34 proves this but best wait until we get to it.

These gentlemen never tell the keys and indications by which they forecast big movements. They are a silent lot. When actively trading, they often shut themselves up away from everybody and do all business by telephone. They have a corps of clerks working over information, securing fresh news, charting the various options while they watch their ticker and give in the orders. The private office of a big trader during a bull market is a scene of intense interest and his chart rooms a center of feverish activity. The trader sends in his orders, then watches their effect upon the market. He seldom works in conjunction with another big trader as it is difficult for independent and powerful speculators to agree. Speculating, like forecasting, is a job in which men work best alone. The lesser traders may work sympathetically on the same side of the market but are not partners in his transactions.

One of the chief points of success in the professional's plan of action is his ability to remain inactive until the correct time arrives. His much desired bull move may not get under way for a year but he waits, knowing the time will surely come. By turning back to page 26 the reader will note that there were **nine bull movements** within the space of six and one-half years. Every one of these felt the active presence of professional traders. Some of them are able to work on both sides of the market, but usually they have a preference for one side and work best on that side.

When preparing a campaign in the stock market the professional secures all information possible about the stocks in which he intends to make his drive. If stocks hold no promise of enhancement he may come over into the wheat market and when he does, he is just as thorough in securing wheat information as he is in checking up on stocks.

A brilliant chapter in the little known history of professional traders, compiled from bulletins issued by the Department of Agriculture, is shown in the graph which follows this page. Big traders are extremely reticent about their deals, but the information given herewith is authentic and becomes extremely useful to the market student. It should be studied carefully as the operations are, in some cases, very shrewdly engineered and at other times they are the disorganized attempts at profit by a confused mind.

It will be remembered that the high top of $2.05⅞ was reached on January 28, 1925. That was the "Coolidge bull market." Quite aside from any special virtue of the president, a second bull move in 1925 developed which made its high top on December 29 at 176½. It is this last move which is pictured in the graph. It had a total advance of 40¼ from the extreme bottom, the entire move being completed in eighty-seven days.

As a side-light on the "vertical rise," which the reader has been studying in the forepart of this book, it is interesting to note the almost straight up rise from November 10 to December 7 and the additional rise from December 22 to December 29. You will remember the return movement law is that the price will eventually return to its starting place (144). On May 29 it is seen the **complete return** has been made.

From the various sharp movements in this eight months period, as charted, it will be seen that vertical rises and vertical breaks are the result of active, heavy trading. It may be taken as a general proposition that most of these straight up or straight down movements are produced by heavy trading. However, there are occasional times when a slow, daily sinking of the market will take place because of **absence** of buying. Such a slow decline occurred in 1931 from July 3 to September 3 in the wheat options. Vertical declines are mostly from forced liquidation of heavy long accounts as occurred several times in the graph on page 34.

The reason the price held relatively strong for six months after top was made was because of **bonehead** plays by the two professionals, as will be shown.

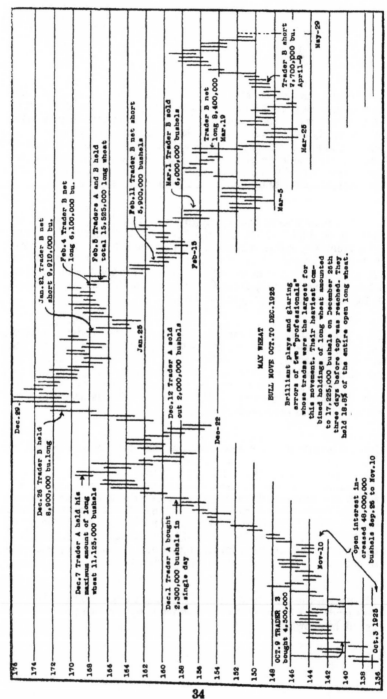

MAY WHEAT

BULL MOVE OCT. TO DEC. 1925

Brilliant plays and glaring
errors of two "professionals"
whose trades were the largest for
this movement. Their heaviest combined holdings of long wheat amounted
to 17,225,000 bushels on December 26th
three days before top was reached. They
held 18.8% of the entire open long wheat.

Dec. 26 Trader B held
8,900,000 bu. long

Dec. 7 Trader A held his
maximum amount of long
wheat 11,125,000 bushels

Dec. 1 Trader A bought
2,300,000 bushels in
a single day

Dec. 12 Trader A sold
out 2,000,000 bushels

Jan. 21 Trader B net
short 9,910,000 bu.

Feb. 4 Trader B net
long 6,100,000 bu.

Feb. 5 Traders A and B held
total 15,525,000 long wheat

Feb. 11 Trader B net short
5,900,000 bushels

Mar. 1 Trader B sold
6,000,000 bushels

Trader B net
long 8,400,000
Mar. 19

Trader B short
7,700,000 bu.
April-9

OCT. 9 TRADER B
bought 4,500,000

Open interest in-
creased 48,000,000
bushels Sep. 26 to Nov. 10

Oct. 3 1925

Dec. 29.

Jan. 26

Feb. 15

Feb-15

Dec-22

Nov-10

Mar-5

Mar-25

May-29

HOW THE PLAYERS PLAYED

After participating in the huge bull market of early 1925, which was followed in a very short time by the sharp break to around $1.36, these skilled market operators, with the fresh scalps of the "Coolidge bull market" dangling at their belts, laid plans to "coach" a new bull market when the crop shortage of 1925 became known. In 1924 the bull move was "put over" because of the 200,000,000 bushels crop loss in Canada. By the fall of 1925 it happened that the United States crop had fallen 200,000,000 bushels below the former year. Therefore, everything was "set" for a fine advance and it began about October 3.

Within a space of fourteen days and in a range of twelve cents from September 26 to November 10, the operators accumulated the initial loads for the expected bull movement. We have only the record of one purchase made in the accumulating zone, but both of these gentlemen must have taken on a lot of wheat as the open interest increased 49,000,000 in the two weeks. Of course, smaller traders were entering the market. One of the signs of a coming advance is an increasing open interest during a sharp decline.

The signal for a rapid rise came as usual when the price advanced above the bottom congestion (see KEY NUMBER ONE in Book II). Doubtless the operators were aware of this key. One trader, the one designated as "B," was so confident of the coming move that he took on 4,500,000 bushels near the bottom as will be noted on October 9. This was doubtless his nest egg and the lot which made him the big money for the bull move. We have no further traces of him until on December 26, when we learn that the two traders, A and B, held a total of 17,225,000 bushels.

This enormous lot of long wheat was held when the market was within five or six cents of the extreme top!

Yet so skillfully was this amount of wheat handled that by January 21 the long wheat had been disposed of and trader B was net short 9,910,000 bushels within nine cents of the top.

35

Trader A was doing some fine work on the upside as the record shows that by December 7 he had accumulated his maximum amount—11,125,000 bushels. Evidently he had been buying all the way up and was feeling pretty sure of a very large advance as he took on 2,300,000 bushels in a single day—December 1.

A sidelight on the opinion of Trader A is shown by the fact that he held his heaviest load at the top of a fourteen cent decline. He seemed to be confident the advance was to go much further—and without much reaction—or he would have been lightening instead of increasing his load prior to the top of December 7. Furthermore, it shows plainly that doubt was beginning to creep into his mind on the two weeks break from December 7 to December 22, for he hastily dumped 2,000,000 bushels in a single day.

Fresh courage came to trader A after dumping that big lot for the reason the market held well during the dumping process. It must have convinced him that a better advance was still to come as we find that by December 26 the two traders held 17,225,000 bushels.

The 2,000,000 bushel sell-out by Trader A on December 12, may look like a bonehead play, but could be quite the opposite. Perhaps he was testing the market to see how much selling it could withstand. He disposed of another million bushels somewhere along the line, but on December 26 he still had 8,100,000 bushels.

Most traders can do well on a bull market, but find the bear market a deception and a snare. The reader will notice how well both of these traders worked on the bull side from the bottom right up to the top. Their errors were few and their profits enormous, but once over to the bear side both of these traders lost their step with the market and began to jump around wildly. In the reader's mind the old adage will be recalled—"Make it in a bull move and lose it in a bear move." There is much truth in it and the reason is not hard to find. Our business in studying the market is to find how errors are made, then take steps to avoid them.

Trader B, on January 21, would have to be commended on his ability to unload long wheat and accumulate a short line of 9,100,000 bushels. He alone was able to sell 18,000,000 bushels not far from top figures. WHY? Because public enthusiasm becomes so strong on big advances that a host of small, ill-advised traders begin to buy to their limit. They absorb wheat rapidly on reactions.

WHOSE FAULT THEN? The fault is in the race itself. This process of rushing into booms at the top and of liquidating every dollar's worth of property at bottom levels is a racial habit. People should know better by the sheer example of the past, but they heed not. This up and down process is always going on. Our people will, in the next bull market, do exactly as they did in the last one. The "professional" belongs to that small class of careful beings who take thought of the market and who make their profits by going opposite to the utterly wrong methods of the small traders.

However, the professional also makes his mistakes. Often he falls into the pit he digs for others. In the record of operations, during the bear market from December 20 to May 29, page 34, is seen a series of profoundly incorrect plays so manifestly bad as to make our student trader shiver. Most of the money made in the bull movement must have been lost in the bear market that followed.

For instance, if these operators had been fully aware of the return movement—as they ought to have been—they would have put out a short line and held it through for the big decline which is fully as certain as the bull move. Our student trader would instantly know that; as the price rose almost vertically from November 10, it would eventually return to that level. It was not at all difficult to pick the top. Both traders did that very neatly. The big surprise is that after they went short they did not stay short!

ON FEBRUARY 4, Trader B was **net long** 6,100,000 bushels and the next day A and B together were **net long** 15,525,000 bushels within ten cents of the top!

Perhaps these two operators were trying for that somewhat evasive phenomena—the "double top." If so, they overlooked the fact that their unloading of over 18,000,000 bushels around top figures chilled the market and paved the way for a complete collapse of the price.

Trader A fades out of the picture here, having evidently become disgusted at his failure to read the market. Trader B, however, had some money left and again set out to beat the market by "in and out" trading on both sides. This, it should be remembered by the student, is the most difficult form of trading and is seldom successful. In and out trading, using one side only, is the perfection of market practice but must be done according to the correct trend. An excellent outline of this is given in the last book of this course. It is well worth the whole set of books.

On February 11 Trader B was going well again. He was short some 5,900,000 bushels. Of course, he had to take a heavy loss on his long line just sold out, but he felt encouraged by March 1 and sold a huge chunk—6,000,000 in one day. Why he did not stick to his line again puzzles us. He could have sold out twelve cents lower by all the laws of market action, but for some unaccountable reason we find him **long** 8,400,000 on March 19, ten cents above bottom.

TO CAP THE CLIMAX of his ill-starred bear market operations, we find him short 7,700,000 bushels after the market had practically made bottom. This mistake must have cost him dearly as the ten cent rapid rise above April 9 was doubtless due to his frantic efforts to get rid of his short wheat.

Thus we come to the close of Book IV. Within its pages are some of the most spectacular as well as useful movements known to market action. It is well to study these types of action along with charts of the options. Sharp breaks or sharp advances are very fruitful of indications. Any big impulse in human affairs brings a train of results. The race does its best work by a series of booms and panics, of bulges and breaks and those who take the pains to understand them are the ones who reap the rewards.

THE TALENT IS THE CALL

"Every man has the call of the power to do something unique, and no man has any other call. By doing his work he makes the need felt which he can supply. He creates the taste by which he is enjoyed. He provokes the wants to which he can minister. By doing his own work he unfolds himself."

—Emerson

BOOK FIVE

THE MOON AND THE MARKET

The moon exerts a strange, indirect but very important influence upon the wheat market.

People turn readily to a study of outside forces, things remote, obscure or mysterious which they may believe has some influence upon their lives especially upon their love affairs and financial matters.

The race must have lived long upon the earth before it began to take on the airs of civilization because we find in human habits the outcroppings of what must have been ancient fears or beliefs. Right at the present time, in remote localities, there are communities which believe that to carry a buckeye or a potato in the pocket will cure rheumatism, that bleeding will cure disease, that a black cat crossing the road is an evil sign or that the number thirteen is to be avoided as omen of bad luck. In China thousands join in parades with grotesque and horrifying forms of stuffed dragons designed to frighten bad spirits away.

The moon influence, which we are now to take up, seems to be a heritage of the race; a faint remnant of the ancient regard of the cave man for the silvery orb that illumined his way through the forest at night and yielded to the mightier sun when dawn crept up from the east. With his adoption of the trapping of civilization he has not abandoned age old ideas. Scientists have been amazed at the thinness of the veneer of culture that makes what we call an educated man. In times of great stress men become ferocious, cowardly, or terror-stricken even as did their progenitors of a half million years back.

The author would prefer not to admit anything in this book that is illogical or not adequately supported by hard scientific facts but years of observation of the markets compel him to accept certain **moon phenomena** as true and useful to the market student. A habit deeply fixed in the race becomes so regular and so powerful as to amount to a law. "Self preservation is the first law of Nature" runs an old adage and it is so true that a man rises to his sublimest heights in his obedience to this law.

Any outside influence recurring frequently will, in time, weave itself into the intimate lives of the people. The Egyptians, Persians,

2

Aztecs and other ancient peoples worshipped the sun because it came into their lives day after day. Sun worship was probably the first form of religion.

The moon influence is gentler. It comes less frequently because of the two intermittent phases, the light of the moon and the dark of the moon. It is difficult to establish any scientific reason for the moon influence, hence we are obliged to fall back upon the habit of the race in giving "power" to any heavenly body or phenomena that seems nearer to the omnipotent fountainhead of power than itself.

So eager are people for information that would assist them in market affairs that they accept unreliable and often very faint indications as if they were fact or truth. Certain astrologers profess to be able to associate human impulses with the activities of the planets. From these planetary influences they make deductions as to the movement of prices. Some of the planets are supposed to be bad or malefic. Others are good or beneficent. How they discovered this is clouded with mystery. A country boy entered college and took up astronomy. When friends asked him how he was getting along he replied: "Fine. I like it, but I'm puzzled sometimes. I can understand how the astronomers can measure the distance to the stars but d - - ned if I can tell how they found out what their names are."

The author of this course has very scant knowledge of astrology. All attempts to align our activities with the far away planets have been fruitless with the sole exception of the moon and its two phases. A record of market action of the several wheat options shows such an important connection with these two phases that they can be used to the advantage of the trader. In fact no trader should be without a knowledge of how the moon affects the market.

A warning must be given here, however, that this moon influence is modest. Its chief power is that it is widespread. It cannot be resolved into a "system" but is necessary in any and all plans and systems. It works so beautifully for months at a time that traders become enthusiastic and adopt a moon phase method as if it were fixed and certain and would work all the time, but this is a mistake. The object of this book is to enable traders to use the phases when they are "in line" with the market and to discard them at other times.

3

THE MOON AND THE HUMAN RACE

As far back as history goes this almost nightly appearing orb has excited curiosity, worship and inspiration in the human race. It is a dead world, devoid of life or surrounding atmosphere, serrated with mountain ranges, dotted with huge craters of extinct volcanoes, gashed with deep canyons and as dry as the sands of Sahara. During high noon, temperatures on the moon run up to 212 and in the night descend to 100 below zero. The satellite has no electrical effect upon the earth and little attention would be paid to it were it not that it brilliantly reflects the rays of the sun, flooding the earth at night with a beautiful, welcome light.

Deep in the minds of our ancestors was planted a reverence for this orb that shone brilliantly for a time then disappeared within its shadow for awhile only to return again. To the savages it was a sort of deity of the darksome night to be worshiped with crude incantations. When it disappeared they wished for its return and when it reappeared they welcomed it. Advancing toward civilization earlier peoples began framing rude ideas as to the meaning of the light moon and the dark moon.

Sacred literature is full of references to the moon and the important part it played in the life of ancient peoples. Jeremiah was sent to make a special appeal to the Jews of Egypt, then the granary of the world, urging them to cease their feasts to the New Moon as their devotion to this pastime began to savor of idolatry. With them the "New Moon" meant Full Moon. They defied Jeremiah and refused to abandon their practices saying they would continue to worship the "queen of the heavens" because they failed to prosper when they ceased this ceremony. Jeremiah lived 2550 years ago but even at that early age the moon habit was deeply imbedded in the race.

Moses abjured the Israelites to leave off their idolatrous worship of the Moon more than 1400 years before the Christian era.

In the famous story of David and Jonathan, King Saul had plotted to slay David at a feast of the New Moon. Jonathan, the son of Saul, "loved David as his own soul" and devised the scheme of shooting the arrows in the field to warn his pal of the danger. This incident happened 1062 years before Christ. The Moon habit still clung to the people.

There is a strange significance in the words of the old prophet Amos where he reprimanded certain wealthy merchants for saying "when will the new moon be gone that we may sell corn?" (Amos 8-5). Of course, Amos meant wheat and it may be mentioned here that wheat shows the most distinct affinity for the moon phases of any commodity.

All through history we find interesting testimony to the deep impression made upon the minds of our ancestors by the beautiful satellite which rides through our heavens now just as it appeared to them in the centuries of long ago.

But still later, coming down at once to times within our own knowledge and memory, we find many intelligent people unshaken in their belief that the moon wields a strange power over the growth of certain vegetation. Since man must live from the products of the soil it is natural that he should associate the phases of the moon with the growth of his life giving crops. Thus it came about that root crops, bulbs, potatoes, mushrooms and crops that produce their fruits in the darkness of the soil were supposed not to need the benefaction of moonlight and thrived best when planted in the **dark of the moon.**

On the other hand wheat, corn and other grains that bear their crops above the ground were supposed to prosper and revel in the **light of the moon.** It is natural that wheat, the world's bread crop, should show the clearest effects of the moon phases but it must be noted that these "effects" are not in yields or quality but in **wheat prices.**

5

Hence we have, coming down to us step by step from time imme-
morial, a strong conviction in the minds of people, a subconscious
heritage of belief in the importance of the light and phases of the
moon. The reader may be surprised to know that our government,
only a few years ago, finding this moon opinion prevalent over wide
sections of the country, conducted a series of exhaustive experiments
to determine whether the moon effects were myths or facts. The
result was that science could see no effect whatsoever but not in
the slightest did it alter the inherent and inherited belief that the
moon phases do have their effect. These ancient beliefs are too
deeply rooted in the race to perish readily. They are imbedded in
the psychology of the race and will take centuries to die out.

It is not to be understood by the student of these lessons that the
effect of the moon upon wheat prices is profound and invariable.
Rather it is explained herein with a view to showing the student
certain times when the phases can be used and when they are extremely important. Out of all of the factors that **shape market
action** there are but a very few that may be successfully used, or
that are really needed, and the two phases of the moon are num-
bered amongst the useful factors. The small daily movements of
the wheat market are caused by the small deals, small thoughts,
and local opinions that enter into the market. The big movements
are the outcome of deeply imbedded psychological factors, most
frequently great fear of loss or high hopes of gain but sometimes
the result of powerful but obscure forces and the moon phases are
of this type.

In the daily grain services issued for years by the author, there
were many of the largest movements which were forecastable **only
by the use of the moon phases.** The skilled operator comes to watch
these phases as carefully as he does crop news or political happenings at Washington. The moon is one of the ingredients out of
which forecasts are compounded.

THE MOON DOWN TO DATE

So important has this strange moon obsession become in the minds of the people that every calendar on your walls that purports to be complete, shows all the changes of the moon. No agriculturist would tolerate a calendar that failed to show the light and dark dates of the satellite. The World's Almanac and all other almanacs describe fully every phase of the orb as though it was of first importance to the almanac reader but little is said about the sun.

When the "change of the moon" is at hand there is a distinct persuasion in the minds of many people that various other changes are due. They expect a change in the weather or perhaps some change in their bodily health and since prices are so highly important in the lives of all people they come to expect some sort of change in the price of the commodities they have to buy. So it occurs that the moon is accredited with a tremendous influence over the affairs of men and it matters little whether these influences are real or inherited or imaginary they have an unmistakable effect on markets that cannot be ignored and therefore are to be used.

Millions of our people look forward to better or worse weather with the change of the moon. Droughts or floods are laid at the door of a "wet moon" or a "dry moon." Storms, frosts and clearing weather are supposed to be under the stimulus or control of this neighboring heavenly body and thus it comes to us inescapably that in the minds of a large portion of our people, either consciously or subconsciously, there is an inherited, persistent, ineradicable belief that the moon, with its light and dark phases, holds strange effect and power over the intimate things of life.

One of the causes of failure in forecasting market movements is an unwillingness on the part of observers to use the "psychology of traders" in their calculations. They attempt to adhere to cold, mathematical statistics. The human mind is impulsive, full of fear, hope, and greed and is little concerned with market figures.

7

HOW THE MOON PHASES WORK

For pages we might continue enumerating Moon effects upon the market but the above brief history of how the race has taken the Moon into its daily life is enough to convince the market student that the two phases of this satellite of the earth must be reckoned with.

Next it is desired to show how the phases affect the market through men, then, still more vital, how to use them to one's personal advantage. The author is neither astrologer or astronomer and has but little belief in the occult or mysterious as being of importance in the movements of the market. Few are the factors in market action that cannot be analyzed. The author's reason for making an important matter of the Moon in the market is that a very close relationship exists at times between the phases of the Moon and the movements of wheat that the trader should by all means know. Strangely enough, there are other times when the wheat market seems to totally ignore the phases and may sometimes move entirely contrary to its usual "Moon habits."

THE EFFECT OF THE MOON is on men, not on wheat itself nor upon any of the manipulations that occur in the transportation or handling of the grain. We find it affecting wheat more intensely than any other commodity, the reason being that bread, the "Staff of Life" is a common need of the whole human race, and since price is the all-important factor the Moon delivers its effect upon the price THROUGH MEN.

The most potent influence in the market is the opinion of men who are trading. What a man believes, he does. If he feels confident of better prices he buys. If he is doubtful, he stays out or if long, he may sell out. When a majority of traders happen to acquire the same opinion and act in unison the market moves strongly in sympathy with that opinion. Statistics, news and crop conditions are powerless against a majority of traders acting in unison.

8

Now we come to the reason. With the coming of the FULL MOON, spreading its beauty and brilliance over the world, famed in sentiment and song and bearing an undercurrent of the age-old Moon beliefs in the subconscious mind of men, **men become optimistic and buy.**

All men may not become optimistic and buy with the coming of the Full Moon but so many more become optimistic and so many more take the long side that it usually TURNS THE TIDE OF THE MARKET UPWARD.

Conversely, when the full moon has run its course (12 to 14 days) and the dark phase enters, **optimism wanes** and an impulse to sell out or sell short takes possession of so many traders that it casts the majority to the **selling side.** Therefore, A DECLINE USUALLY OCCURS.

Summing up the action of the market under the two phases we may state in two brief rules:

> Beginning near the FULL MOON date the wheat market
> is strongly inclined to advance.
> Beginning near the DARK MOON date the wheat market
> is strongly inclined to decline.

This simple statement would seem to make wheat trading so easy that the student will immediately ask, "does the market always follow the moon phases?"

NO, the movements of the wheat options are not always in accord with the moon phases but most of the larger movements **are** in accord with them. These moon effects are not mathematical like the dates of the calendar but are based upon the **psychology of traders** and therefore cannot be measured definitely nor do they always produce a strong enough force to govern the market.

The student will now understand that the moon delivers its effect upon the trader who in turn produces an effect upon the wheat market by the simple operation of buying or selling. At times the public mass is puzzled, confused, doubtful, annoyed or resentful over business or market conditions and its **equanimity** being destroyed, the moon phases for the time lose their effect.

9

NOT ONE TRADER IN A HUNDRED thinks of the moon in making his deals or even notices what phase is in force. It is the general optimism that is in him, or the pessimism, engendered by outside forces and often his inspiration comes from the old, almost submerged, ancient moon complex that harks back to his ancestral days.

Thus the moon effects are mild. They are gently, almost imperceptibly persuasive. The phases gain their power by widespread effect since they touch men in all lands and thus mildly affect world markets. They are so mild that they lose their effect during times of sudden or great stress. A declaration of war between two great nations or a killing hot wave or withering dust storm over wheat countries will completely upset the harmony of the market with the phases FOR A TIME.

Astonishingly soon the options will fall in line with the phases again or will show enough obedience to them to the extent that they can be used to great advantage. The author again warns the student that, fascinating as this moon effect is, it has serious variations and must be used observingly. In the pages which follow every important variation is shown and the reason given why. Then the student is shown the styles of market action in which the two phases deliver their maximum effect and how they may be used to the greatest advantage.

THE AUTHOR of this course uses the phases unceasingly. At times they afford no help. At other times they form the only means by which an important move can be forecasted. The moon is not an independent method of forecasting movements but is of high value in locating the turning points.

THE CHART WHICH FOLLOWS gives the student his first graphic view of the normal action of the two phases when the public is not worried or confused and when the market is taking its natural course. The chart on page 11 is a picture of several small swings working in perfect harmony with the phases. Farther on will be seen a graph in which every dark and light phase of the moon for eight months followed the phases perfectly, fifteen successive swings.

10

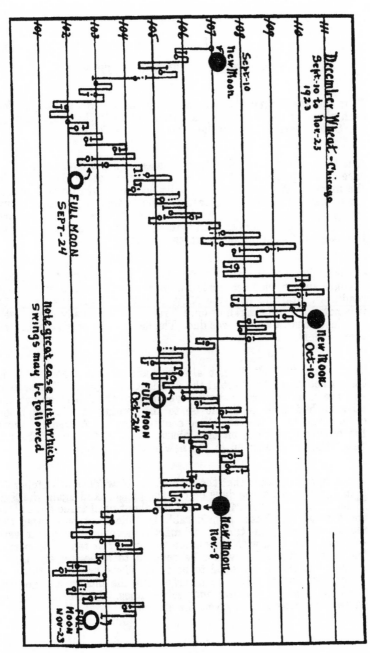

December Wheat - Chicago
Sept.-10 to Nov.-23
1923

Sept-10

New Moon

New Moon
Oct-10

FULL MOON
SEPT-24

FULL MOON
Oct-24

New Moon
Nov-8

FULL MOON
NOV-23

note great ease with which
swings may be followed.

11

TEN WEEKS OF "MOON ACTION"

That there is a very distinct impulse given the wheat market for each phase of the moon is apparent as shown in the chart on page 11. Other charts will show the same general effects.

It is to be remembered that these phases do not deliver their influence in lightning-like strokes, causing sharp or sudden turns in the market. The mind of the public does not turn quickly unless some sharp, exciting event occurs. That's why we have so many swing bottoms covering a week or more of time. It is necessary for the mass of traders to change its opinion or rather the majority to change before a distinct turn can occur.

Occasionally events will occur almost on the day of the moon changes and on such occasions the market will respond with great readiness. Starting with the NEW MOON of Sept. 10 on page 11 it is noted the drop began at once. Traders were already pretty well convinced that a decline was due. The dark phase only accentuated their belief.

That these "turns" do not always come on the moon dates is clearly shown on the chart at the Full Moon of Sept. 24. The bottom and the turn had occurred six days prior to the full moon yet the advance had been negligible up to the coming of the full moon date. Then the price rose three cents promptly. A trader, basing his buying operations on this phase, would get most of the advance that continued up to the new moon of October 10.

Again it will be noted that the turn at the New Moon of October 10 actually occurred three days before the phase. And again the Full Moon turn of October 24 did not come about until three days after the date of the phase. Considerable latitude must be allowed the market in making the turn. If all market movements of wheat were as closely in accord with the phases as during this ten weeks period the matter of trading would be reduced to an extremely simple matter, but this is too good to be true. There are other times at which the market seems to utterly flout the phases and go contrary to them for several successive times. A careful study of these exceptions will be given the student.

12

DO THE MOON PHASES AFFECT OTHER GRAINS?

The phases affect other grains indirectly. On page 15 a graph is shown picturing the apparent effect of the full moon and the new moon on corn. It is readily seen that advances take place in corn around full moon dates, just as in wheat, and that declines follow the new moon. By referring to the chart on page 11 you will see the same period in wheat. The reason corn comported itself so well with the phases is because corn was following wheat, which is its usual custom. Should wheat at times travel adversely to the moon phases, corn also will travel adversely to them. The reason wheat is more obedient to the moon phases than any of the other grains is because of its widespread use, being a native crop of many countries and used by nearly all peoples of the world.

Corn is more largely grown in the United States than in any other country. It is to that extent a local crop. We produce four-fifths of the world's corn and use nearly all of it ourselves. We produce about one-fourth of the world's wheat and export some of that. Corn does not feel the effects of trading in foreign nations like wheat does. Since the moon effects are produced through a mild mass psychology they do not affect corn directly. The swings in corn are merely imitations of wheat swings.

New York stocks show some inclination to follow the moon phases, especially those stocks traded in by foreign countries which thus adds their mass of business to our own. Yet even the best of them, or the most popular of the stocks do not follow the phases with nearly the accuracy that is found in the wheat options. U. S. Steel perhaps comes the nearest to obeying the phases of any stock and this is because of its wide popularity and the constantly heavy volume of trading in this issue.

Stock traders, however, will find the moon phases of little value in forecasting stock movements. The moon more readily affects the agricultural line than the industrial line.

Other grains, such as rye, barley and oats, are also more imitators of wheat than followers of the moon phases. For that reason there are no charts given showing the effects of the phases in the other grains, with the sole exception of the corn chart on page 15, which is intended to show how corn indirectly follows the phases through wheat.

The student's greatest difficulty is going to be not to become too closely attached to the moon method. It is so easy when it is working correctly that it scarcely takes an active thought, to make a deal and close it. But there are exceptions which are extremely important and in which the moon phases apparently fail to work but in reality are working in a different way.

One of the apparent exceptions will be given you, both in this book (Number V) and also in book VI. This exception deals with bull markets but that will come on a later page. The principal thing for us to learn now is that the moon phases are to be used for their great convenience but that the operator must understand the cause of adverse moves, the times when wheat fails to move upward to the full phase or downward to the dark phase. There are instances, though very few, in which a full moon phase occurs at the extreme top of a swing or the dark moon phase will occur at the extreme bottom which is exactly the reverse of where they should be.

Sometimes the market seems to get out of step with the phases for a time moving part of the time with the phase, then reversing in the middle of the phaes. Such irregularities are attributable to a confused state of mind of the public anxious, worried or dissatisfied with some condition in the country.

While these times of irregularity are usually righted after one or two phases go wrong, yet they are so frequent that the trader needs to be constantly on the lookout. When the phases go wrong then fall back upon other methods shown in this course. All through this trading the student should use a combination of the market habits and rules found in this course.

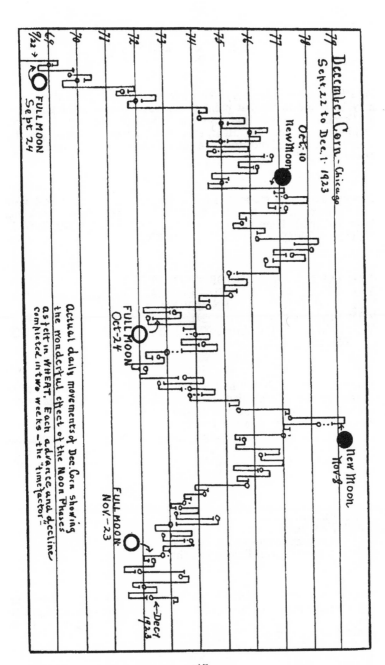

December Corn – Chicago
Sept. 22 to Dec. 1 1923

Oct. 10
New Moon

New Moon
Nov 8

FULL MOON
Oct. 24

FULL MOON
Nov. 23

FULL MOON
Sept. 24

9/22 →

←Dec 1
1923

Actual daily movements of Dec. Corn showing
the wonderful effect of the Moon Phases
as left in WHEAT. Each advance and decline
completed in two weeks – the "time factor."

15

A POWERFUL COMBINATION

MARKET LAWS are very few. Scores of small ineffectual rules may be found in market publications but money cannot be risked on them. Remember that great as Nature is, her important laws or phenomena are few. Heat, cold, light, darkness, wind, gravitation, lightning and moisture are the things by which human beings are most readily affected.

In this course the student is being taught the few very best laws and phenomena known to the market. Up to the present book you have had, aside from the simple but useful KEYS NUMBER ONE, NUMBER TWO and NUMBER THREE:

THE INVALUABLE MINOR TREND LINE
THE VERTICAL RISE AND VERTICAL DECLINE.
THE UNFAILING RETURN MOVEMENT.
THE LONG ECONOMIC TRENDS.
THE SUBTLE BUT ALWAYS PRESENT MOON PHASE EFFECTS.

Last and best of all will be the Bull and Bear Market Laws, to be shown, proven and applied in the last book (Book VI) and which are worth more than the cost of the entire course.
Now there are times when two of these—or even three—happen to deliver their force in a single direction. When this occurs, the expected movement is almost as certain as the laws of Nature.
For instance when you are watching a wheat movement you might have:

A vertical rise.
A New Moon at the top.
The return movement pulling downward.
The minor trend line to tell the turn.

With such a combination as this—and there are many of them during a year's movements—the trader can take unbelievable profits from the market if he will but observe the necessary precautions against overtrading.

16

WAIT FOR A POSITION

Select positions are the most profitable. It pays to wait for them. If you try to be in the market all the time you will be sure to be "tied up" just when there is a fine opportunity at hand. Wait until you can catch the market in a "strained" position. Then it is easy to handle. It will work for you. You can go with it because it has to make a certain return and you catch it "away from home."

Looking back over the July wheat chart now in force (1932) the student can see nine vertical rises and breaks in eight months time. Every one of them caught the market in a vulnerable position, at a strain, and in a hurry to get back again. A strained position in the market is when it has gone too far against a market law.

Wheat prices are ceaselessly trying to strike a level that will satisfy supply and demand. When these prices run too far above the normal level of supply and demand they become stretched like rubber and are eventually pulled back down into line again. A vertical break stretches the price downward too far and the result is that the market is pulled back up into line again.

When the market is simply meandering along undulating slowly and within comparatively narrow limits—say four to six cents—there are no vertical rises or vertical breaks, no return movements to be made, and no minor trends. There is nothing to do but wait for indications. Out of a dull market a bull market may spring but that comes later. While the crop conditions are getting shaped up for a bull move there are numbers of very excellent positions developing that will yield welcome and ample profits. On an average of once a month during reasonably active markets one of these favored positions will develop. The wise trader will wait for them then and take his profits with certainty.

On the next page is an excellent graph of recent wheat action showing the way the moon phases affect the market and how powerful combinations of market forces are at times available.

17

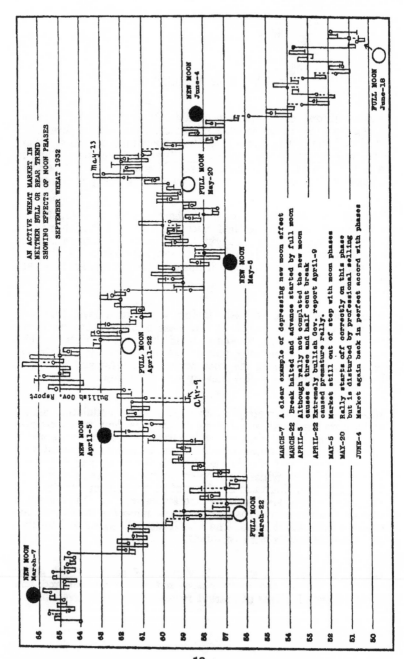

AN ACTIVE WHEAT MARKET IN
NEITHER BULL OR BEAR TREND
SHOWING EFFECTS OF MOON PHASES

SEPTEMBER WHEAT 1932

NEW MOON
March-7

NEW MOON
April-5

FULL MOON
March-22

FULL MOON
April-22

NEW MOON
May-5

FULL MOON
May-20

NEW MOON
June-4

FULL MOON
June-18

Bullish Gov. Report

May-23

MARCH-7   A clear example of depressing new moon effect
MARCH-22   Break halted and advance started by full moon
APRIL-5   Although rally not completed the new moon
           causes a three and half cent break
APRIL-22   Extremely bullish Gov. report April-9
           caused premature rally.
MAY-5   Market still out of step with moon phases
MAY-20   Rally starts off correctly on this phase
           but is disturbed by professional selling
JUNE-4   Market again back in perfect accord with phases

18

The September wheat chart on page 18 clearly shows the way
the moon phases deliver their effect upon wheat options and how,
at times, something more effective than they will completely upset
moon action. Remember the beginning of the new moon phase
normally causes a decline. The full moon phase normally causes
an advance.

BECAUSE MOON EFFECTS ARE MILD IT OFTEN
HAPPENS THAT EXCITING OR POWERFUL NEWS
WILL INFLUENCE THE MARKET MORE THAN THE
PHASES AND WILL TURN PRICES DIRECTLY
AGAINST PHASE ACTION.

On March 7 the market fell into perfect line with the new moon
phase and broke to the 56-57 level by the time the full moon came
in. The coming of the full moon halted the break and after a few
days workout—as often happens—the normal advance started.

On March 22 the full moon started the advance properly and by
April 5 the price was up six cents. The incoming new moon stopped the advance and in four days (from April 5 to April 9) forced
a break of over three and one-half cents. The new moon was
delivering its usual depressing effect when the very bullish Government report of April 9 came out proclaiming a loss of 340,000,000
bushels of winter wheat under last year's crop. The rise to 66¾
followed and was against the new moon phase. This is an instance
when disturbing outside news was stronger than the milder phase
effects.

TWO POWERFUL FORCES WERE UNITING TO
CAUSE THE ADVANCE FROM 56. THE FULL MOON
AND THE "RETURN MOVEMENT." THE RETURN
MOVEMENT FOLLOWED THE VERTICAL BREAK
FROM 64½ AND PROVED MORE POWERFUL THAN
THE NEW MOON PHASE.

April 22 shows the market out of step with the phases having been
completely upset by the bullish Government report of April 9. By
May 20 the market was in step again and by June 4 professional
market operators were selling the market down preparatory to
staging an advance. They began selling May 31, thus preventing
the completion of the full moon advance which started on May 20.

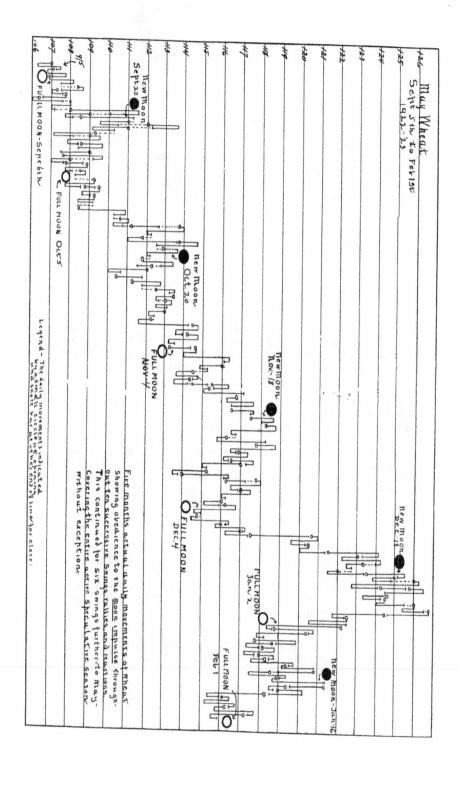

May Wheat
Sept 5th to Feb 15t
1922 - 23

New Moon
Sept 20

Full Moon
Oct 5

New Moon
Oct 20

Full Moon
Nov 4

New Moon
Nov 18

Full Moon
Dec 4

New Moon
Dec 18

Full Moon
Jan 2

New Moon Jan 16

Full Moon
Feb 1

Full Moon Sept 6th

Legend - The daily movements indicated
by a short horizontal line at the opening
which is not carried through until close.

Five months actual daily movements of Wheat
showing obedience to the Moon impulse throughout ten successive swings, rallies and reactions.
This continued for six swings further to May-
covering the entire active speculative season
without exception.

MOON PHASES IN DRIFTING MARKETS

The style of market which most readily follows moon phases is the period of drifting movements which prevails while wheat is between the ending of a bear market and the beginning of the next aggressive bull market. The student has learned that when a bull market is ended a bear market immediately begins and at the end of a bear market a bull market immediately begins. However, there is a period of undulating movements sometimes developing into sharp swings which follows a bear market and these swings are often in perfect harmony with the phases. An example of this kind of market is given on pages 21 and 22. Such a movement may be followed with great ease by the use of the phases and nothing else.

The student trader will be impatient at the beginning of a phase if the movement does not begin at once but it should be rememberd that a phase is really several days in ending and beginning the next phase. However it often happens that a sharp day or two days advance is topped by a new moon date. In such cases it is time to sell out long wheat and take the short side. (One exception to this to be shown later). A sharp, quick break to the full moon date is usually the end of the break. It is then time to buy wheat.

Referring back to the chart on page 18 the rise to May 23 came correctly but professional traders began selling wheat heavily to dislodge the heavy long interest and force a break which could be utilized for buying wheat on a large scale. It is an old habit of professionals to start a strong move by first depressing the price to bargain levels. They buy the wheat which longs are forced to sell out because of weak margins. This was not adequately explained on page 19.

During quiet years, when the country is not torn with political dissensions, or distressed by discord or crop worries, the moon phases are very effective. The market moves in reasonably accurate step with the phases. There are many accurate phase movements even in distressed times but the market is likely to turn suddenly and move directly opposite to the phase for awhile.

THE MOON AN ACCESSORY, NOT A METHOD

While there are many times when the phase movements may be followed with great profit there are too many exceptions to permit the trader to use them constantly. The best way to study and use them is to mark up on your chart the moon dates as we have shown in the various charts. The author uses them carefully in all market predictions but always with the knowledge that any phase may form an exception. If everything seems to move off nicely with a break following the new moon or a bulge following the full moon then we fully expect the next phase to turn the market again. The use of the phases along with the vertical movements is particularly effective.

WAIT UNTIL A VERTICAL BREAK has run to the **full moon date** and you will see the market halt preparatory to a rise. If the break has been sharp the advance will be correspondingly sharp. **Persons who are "natural buys" should wait for such breaks before buying, then buy on the full moon date. Persons who are "natural bears" should wait for a vertical rise, then sell on the new moon date.**

Market action represents a continuous battle between the "in and outers" and the long pull traders. The "in and outers" are continually loking for small indications that furnish a reason for a one or two cent rally or a similar break. There is such a large majority trading this way and it answers the needs of the broker so well that newspaper comment and brokerage house bulletins dwell too much upon these small indications. The long pull trader or the swing trader is by far the most successful in aggregate profits but he has to continually fight against misleading small indications.

That's why anything that will indicate an important turn or a swing turn is so useful. It enables the long pull trader to buy or sell short near the beginning of an extensive move. The moon phases furnish several very excellent turns every year.

It is the aim of this course of market study to induce the trader to wait patiently for decisive turns. We cannot inpress upon him too earnestly the value of the vertical rise or the vertical break. They occur with great frequency. They cause the amateur to sell at the bottom of a break because he incorrectly believes it is going lower. It also induces the same amateur to buy wheat at the top of a vertical rise because he believes the market is going still higher. This unfortunate mistake by public traders plays directly into the hand of the market student or the professional trader. Let us put it briefly:

A vertical break traps the shorts and forces a sharp advance on short covering.

A vertical rise traps the longs and forces a break or what is known in the market as a "shakeout."

The moon phases are nearly always found to be correct on these vertical movements. A very excellent movement of this kind bgan after March 7, the new moon phase in 1932 as shown on page 18 and another one on June 4. They are worth waiting for. When prices are low, as they were during the first half of 1932, wheat is a gold mine for any trader who uses ordinary business sense. It is evident that with wheat far below the cost of production, prices cannot remain down and cannot go much lower. Therefore, a vertical break of a few cents at any time when wheat is around the 60-50 level was certain of a correspondingly quick advance. At the time of this writing, Chicago July wheat is at 48c or near the lowest prices ever known for wheat futures. Wheat, bought and properly margined at this level, is as sure of rendering a profit as the most skillfully managed merchandising or real estate deal.

Now we are coming to a very brilliant part played by the moon phases in the wheat market. We have reference to the effect of the phases on bull markets., how they operate, how you can tell the beginning of a bull move and the way the movement is prospering under the effect of the phases. All of the phase movements shown you heretofore in this book are for the purpose of proving that the moon delivers an effect upon the wheat market that is very useful and cannot be ignored. Now we come to that climax in moon effects, THE MOON AND THE BULL MARKET.

THE MOON AND THE BULL MARKET

THE MOON PHASES play an extraordinary part in all bull markets of wheat. The full moon starts them off and the new moon tops them out.

There are two styles of bull wheat markets: the short, quick "six weeks bull move" and the longer bull moves of from three to seven months. The six weeks type occurs most frequently and almost every such movement is closely within the limits of three moon phases as will be described.

Book VI of this course deals specifically with bull and bear movements and is the most important book of the set but since the phases play such an important part in bull movements it will be necessary to anticipate some of the things that will be mentioned in Book VI.

ALMOST EVERY BULL MOVE STARTS WITH OR NEAR THE FULL MOON PHASE.

ALMOST EVERY BULL MOVE TOPS OUT AROUND THE NEW MOON PHASE.

This is extremely important information for the trader who believes conditions justify a bull move and wishes to know where to buy into the market. It is just as important that he know how long he should hold his long wheat. This is the simplest and most effective method known of buying at the bottom and taking profits at the top.

In making the start it is essential that the trader watch carefully to see if the movement continues on up **through** and above the next new moon. If it is merely a swing and not a bull move the advance will die out around the new moon phase and the market decline. It will then likely postpone the move for another month.

LARGE OPERATORS, either intentionally or accidentally, use the phases as their early buying operations are synchronous with the full moon and their selling at the top is synchronous with the new moon phase.

THE MOON PHASE EFFECT upon bull wheat markets may be stated briefly as follows:

For the "six weeks bull moves:"

> A bull movement starts with the full moon phase. It continues slowly upward for the first two weeks to—
> the next new moon phase, where it usually halts temporarily, but the public, becoming strongly bullish, forces the price up through the new moon phase in a few days and on up irregularly to—
> the next full moon phase (a month from the start) where the advance, having the doubled power of the bullish public and the new moon, becomes very rapid. It rushes upward another two weeks to make a top at—
> the next new moon phase, or very near the phase where the bull market ends and the bear market sets in.

In the above four short paragraphs the student has the complete effect of the moon upon the six weeks bull moves.

The longer moves, of from three to seven months, start with the full moon in perfect fashion but have a part way reaction from each successive new moon. Every full moon phase drives the market higher than the previous one until finally the finishing or climactic advance takes place. The top will be around or near the new moon phase.

The balance of this book could be filled with graphs of bull movements in which the moon plays its part accurately as described above. There is room for only a few. They are all practically alike except for two occasional mild irregularities. First a dip of two or three cents right after the date of the full moon that is starting a bull move, and second, the advance may be carried a little beyond the new moon date at the top or may stop a day or two prior to the new moon. The author knows of no more useful or welcome information to the bull market wheat trader than how the phases may thus be used.

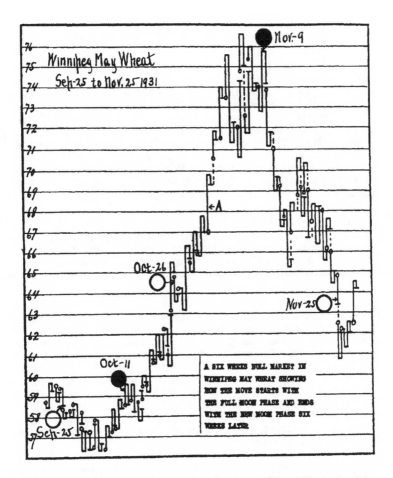

Winnipeg May Wheat
Sep-25 to Nov. 25 1931

Nov-9

←A

Oct-26

Nov-25

Oct-11

Sep-25

A SIX WEEKS BULL MARKET IN
WINNIPEG MAY WHEAT SHOWING
HOW THE MOVE STARTS WITH
THE FULL MOON PHASE AND ENDS
WITH THE NEW MOON PHASE SIX
WEEKS LATER.

A "SIX WEEKS BULL MOVE" in Winnipeg May Wheat is shown above. It is a small move but, in all respects, was like the larger movements that occur when prices are high. Note the small dip in price after the entry of the full moon phase Sept. 25 does not spoil the move. The first two weeks from Sept. 25 to October 11 are very slow. After the full moon phase October 26 the advance is very rapid, reaching top four days ahead of the new moon phase, November 9.

THE MOON AND THE WINNIPEG MARKET

Bull wheat markets and moon effects are the same the world over. North America produces the most export wheat and, having more wheat speculators than the entire balance of the world, whatever movements develop in wheat at Chicago will develop sympathetically in all other markets. The charted bull move on page 27 in Winnipeg May Wheat is simply a duplicate of the bull move at Chicago that started at the same time. Anyone using this course in Canada can make his trades in Winnipeg wheat and follow the moon phases or any of the other market laws given herein as readily as if he were trading in Chicago wheat.

On page 25, near the bottom of the page, mention is made of two occasional mild variations of the moon phase action. They do not in any way disturb or prevent the movement but the trader must know them to avoid confusion.

On September 25 the full moon phase started the bull move on its way but not until a two cent dip to 56¼ cents had occurred. In Chicago May wheat the dip was three cents and the first two weeks between the full moon and dark moon phases were very slow. When the price went up strongly through the new moon phase of October 11 the trading public felt a great exhilaration, an intensified bullishness. Very few of them knew of these moon effects but they are unconsciously inspired by them just the same. Up and up the price goes. Reactions are small. Professionals know there will be a fast climax, a rapid rise, at the end of the advance and buy heavily on all reactions.

THE FULL MOON PHASE of October 26 is a signal that the "fireworks" are about to begin. Note the higher closings each day until at A the market throws off all restraint and rushes upward to complete the move. Bullish optimism becomes rampant during the last full moon phase of a bull wheat market and carries the price far too high. The more pessimistic new moon phase, coming at the top of an over-extended rise, easily stops the advance and turns the market downward. Note the new moon on November 9.

28

So many other graphs of bull movements are shown in the preceding books and in the book to follow that we can save valuable space here by referring to them rather than reproducing them here. Every important type of grain market movement is shown in the set of six books which covers the last ten years or from 1922 to 1932. The reader might chart movements back for fifty years and he would not be able to understand the market better nor would he find any kind of usable market action not pictured and explained in the course. The charts you have been studying are taken from actual daily movements of the options. They are correct and are fully representative. What the market did five or ten years ago or what it did yesterday will be repeated over and over again as long as a futures market is in existence.

Turning to the graph on page 6 of Book Two you will see a six weeks bull move in wheat for the year 1927. The student has already learned the use of the KEY for forecasting this strong move but the moon phases render additional and very excellent help in confirming the move and following it to the top.

HOW WOULD THE TRADER FOLLOW THE MOVE?

He would first buy wheat when it was between A and B as it is bullish when it gets above the bottom congestion. He notes that the moon is "helping" him. At the first dark moon (at C) he notes the price climbs right on up through the phase and knows that a powerful advance is in progress. He holds his wheat. When the advance becomes rapid after the full moon date (wheat on line 132) the trader knows the price will continue advancing rapidly for TWO WEEKS LONGER and will top out around the new moon phase of May 30.

Thus the student trader has the moon phases and KEY NUMBER ONE both helping him. He is able to secure almost the entire move and later lessons will show him how to profit immensely on the downward movement that follows. There is nothing in market science so valuable as knowing how to anticipate and follow a big movement from beginning to the end.

WHERE MOON PHASES ARE MOST USEFUL

THERE ARE TWO very important types of market movement in which the two phases play an important part and in fact, are almost indispensable to the active trader. They are:

First—The six weeks bull movement.
Second—The vertical rise and the vertical break.

Long drawn-out bull movements do not follow the phases so accurately. The student will observe in Book VI the 1924-1925 bull movement which covered seven months. A protracted bull movement such as this becomes a series of big swings and enough discordant influences enter the market to upset the accurate working of the phases. Fortunately for the trader the six weeks type of bull move is far more frequent than the long ones. Out of the last eleven bull moves nine were of the six weeks kind.

Another method of estimating the top for a long drawn out bull move is given in the last book. It is surpisingly simple and takes the place of the moon phases in locating the distant top.

A BULL MOVEMENT IN CORN is shown on page nine of Book Two. While the movement starts off in excellent shape in the full moon phase it terminates in thirty days with the full moon at the top. This goes to show that the phases are most applicable to wheat and that corn, being mostly a U. S. speculative commodity, is too local to adhere closely to the phases. In this corn movement it is entirely clear to the trader that when the advance runs through the new moon phase at C the market is headed for a further big rise. The only thing he doesn't know is that the move may stop anywhere from sheer top-heaviness. Again we must resort to the Book VI method of estimating the top. This is called the BULL MARKET RULE and is one of the most useful methods in determining the end of a bull market far ahead of its top. This corn chart is mentioned to show you corn does not follow the phases unless there is a bull wheat market moving with it. Nevertheless there is a way to compute or estimate the top of even this rapid-fire corn movement.

On page 18 of Book Two is a graph of a three months bull move which started out uncertainly but was helped by spring crop damage to the extent that it developed into a full-fledged bull move. The drawing out of the movement permitted confusion of traders and conflicting reports as to the condition of the new crop. Therefore, it may be said that:

A six weeks bull move rushes through to completion within three moon phases.

A protracted bull move starts its course approximately in conformity with the phases but tops out in either phase.

In following what appears to be a steadily developing bull wheat movement the trader should watch the new moon phase very carefully. If the reaction is small during this phase and the price soon rises above the new moon date then his move is prospering, and he can hold through for another month to the next new moon phase. The 1927-1928 bull market on page 18 of Book Two really and correctly topped out on the "official" new moon date when the price reached 159 but professional speculators engaged in a battle with each other, driving the price up to 171 and forcing the shorts to cover their short wheat.

On page 34 of Book IV is found another bull wheat movement which started September 26 and ran full three months to its finish. This move also started correctly in the full moon phase but was disturbed by a battle of the bulls in which some of them were forced to cover rapidly on the rise from December 22 to December 29. This movement is almost exactly like the 1927-1928 movement.

The lesson for the student trader to draw is that the moon phases are highly useful in getting in near the start of a bull movement and that most of the movements will be completed within six weeks. Movements that become drawn out affairs may lose their step with the moon phases but usually continue to greater heights.

31

On page 23, of Book II, the reader will observe a recent six weeks' bull movement which ran to its top on November 9 in perfect form with the moon phases. Again on page 11, of Book II, will be seen a sympathetic movement of Chicago May Rye that also starts with the full moon phase and ends on the date of the new moon six weeks later. In Book VI are found other examples of a bull movement started off by the full moon phase and finished with a dark moon around extreme top figures six weeks later. The effects of this satellite are too important and too useful to be ignored. This sympathy of the market with the moon phases is real because the human race is sympathetic with that illustrious orb. In conclusion, we may say that the appeal in the moon to the race is little more than Nature speaking to her children.

THE MYSTERIOUS MOON

The effect of the moon upon the human race is as brilliant as its own fascinating light. It sails in stately beauty in an ocean of bottomless blue. The ancients worshipped it. Modern races revel in its nocturnal beauty. Its mellowed radiance rests like a benediction upon sleeping nature and mends the troubled hearts of human beings as the balm of Gilead. The sun dazzles; the moon fascinates. The sun withers; while the moon soothes. Serene and beautiful is a balmy moonlit night. The trees drenched in fathomless moonlight, the grass trembling with crystal dew and the night wind scented with the breath of myriad sleeping flowers brings the human soul to its nearest approach to nature's illimitable heart. Herds that pant in the shade during the heated day graze contentedly in the cool, fair light of this somnolent orb. It is not a planet, not a star, not a sun. Yet in sweet solemnity it delivers a beneficient effect upon the human race today, just as it did upon our humble progenitors ten thousand years ago.

"PRICE MILEAGE"

The most notable thing about wheat prices is their incessant travels. The market is as restless as the sea. The distance an option travels during a few months of dull movements is amazing. The undulations of the market sometimes become so slow that traders claim they cannot make any money, yet if the actual "mileage" of these movements were recorded they would astonish the observer.

A man of experimental turn of mind placed a pedometer (a small machine that registers how far a person walks) in the pocket of a nine year old boy, along with his marbles, to get an idea of the boy's activities. It was found that the little fellow, without attempting to go anywhere, actually traveled eleven miles. In the fabled race of the hare and the tortoise, the hare doubtless lived up to his reputation for speed, while he was in action, but in the end he and the tortoise made the same mileage.

The amateur's chief difficulty, and it often extends to others more experienced, is to prevent the market from changing his mind for him. When a break is on the trader becomes so thoroughly convinced that it is going lower that he unwittingly sells "at the bottom." When the market is advancing he becomes inordinately bullish and too often buys "at the top." This is so common as to be a market joke and yet it is a serious matter because it is one which the trader can break only with extreme determination.

Our much talked about bull markets in wheat cover only about twenty-five per cent of the actual movements of the market. The other seventy-five per cent of the time wheat is meandering, swinging or reeling about in a confused manner with apparently no better understanding of its destination than the overloaded tippler staggering down the street. It is to this very important period which we now wish to have our readers devote their attention for the remaining pages of this book. You have gone through the moon phases and have found how wonderfully they assist in following bull movements, now it is well worth your while to find the method of using the market during the seventy-five per cent of the time it is **NOT IN A BULL MOVE.**

TURN SLOW MOVEMENTS INTO QUICK CASH

Ninety per cent of all active traders attempt to follow the market in both directions. When it is on the upgrade they buy wheat and the farther it has advanced the more aggressively they buy. They follow exactly the same tactics on the down side. It is an unfortunate habit and hard to break. Primarily this error is made because the trader does not understand the trend.

As shown in Book II, trend is a very important matter and is also quite simple. TREND IS DOWN FROM THE TOP OF A BULL MARKET TO THE BOTTOM OF A BEAR MARKET. THEN IT REVERSES AND REMAINS IN UPTREND UNTIL THE NEXT BULL MARKET MAKES TOP.

There is often a long period of undulating movements while a market is preparing to fulfill a trend. For instance on page 23 of Book II, a small bull move is charted which is followed by a break to Nov. 27. From this last date onward to the following July (when this was written) the price of wheat rambled aimlessly, with many excellent swings between 50 and 64, sometimes exceeding these figures slightly. This period of seven months was highly remunerative to the trader who followed the "mileage" plan suggested herewith. This same method has been placed before the student in the Multi-Profit Plan in Book III, but is supplemented now with a graph devised to show the incessant travels of a "dull" market, and how these meandering movements may be turned into money.

When the trader determines the trend definitely—and it is not difficult—he can follow the Multi-Profit Plan with security and the utmost satisfaction. Profits come steadily. They may not be large at first, but if the bull trend is followed faithfully to its climax, then the bear trend, followed as faithfully to its bottom, the amount of profits doubling and trebling would soon amount to an amazing sum.

A FINE RULE for safe margins would be to margin all trades 50% of the value of the wheat. Thus wheat bought at 60 would be margined to 30, but be right with the trend.

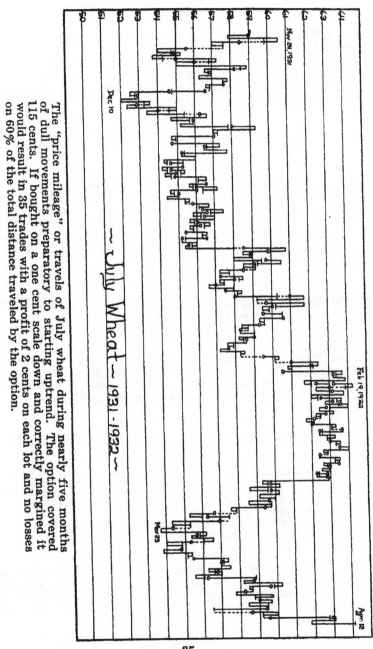

~ July Wheat ~ 1931-1932 ~

Nov. 24, 1931

Dec 10

Feb. 19, 1932

Mar. 23

Apr. 12

The "price mileage" or travels of July wheat during nearly five months of dull movements preparatory to starting uptrend. The option covered 115 cents. If bought on a one cent scale down and correctly margined it would result in 35 trades with a profit of 2 cents on each lot and no losses on 60% of the total distance traveled by the option.

35

SMALL VERTICAL RISES and vertical breaks appear frequently during the period charted on page 35 with a very considerable break from February to March. All of these vertical movements are highly useful in determining the next small swing but trading according to the Multi-Profit Plan is more a matter of placing orders and taking profits than of forecasting the small movements.

SHALL THE TRADER BUY OR SELL HERE? (Chart on page 35)

Every trade should be a purchase. WHY? Because the market has undergone a bear move since the top at 73¼ November 9, and the price is back nearing the original bottom level which was at 49 for July wheat. Therefore, the market is maneuvering in preparation for the next bull move and any lot of wheat bought is sure to make a profit. Also ANY LOT OF WHEAT SOLD SHORT MIGHT BECOME A SURE LOSS.

At the bottom of a bear market buy on a one or two cent scale down and take profits of two cents on each lot.

At the finish of a bull market sell wheat short on a one or two cent scale up on rallies and take two or three cents profit on each lot. The market is so much more active after the finish of a bull move that many trades will easily yield a three cent profit.

WHAT IS MOST DIFFICULT IN THE MULTI-PROFIT PLAN?

Your hardest job will be with yourself to keep from the old inborn habit of overtrading. You will think, "well, this time I know just what to do, I'll buy a big lot and take a heavy profit, and then drop back to the regular plan." That's the voice of doom. If you lay out a plan of action, then surrender to the old enemy, it will be that much harder to reopen your plan again.

The author has known men of large means, who could margin a million bushels of wheat to the limit of absolute safety, who lost their money because they had no fixed plan or policy. They tried to follow both sides. One loss followed another and their fortunes dwindled away.

MERCHANDISING IN WHEAT FUTURES

This is not an exaggerated title. It can be realized to the great delight and profit of the speculator and with as much certainty of gain as if he were selling desirable goods over a counter.

STARTING with 59 on the chart on page 35, the trade should buy wheat at any one cent level down. Buy on each cent because it is easier to figure and just as good as if you bought at fractions of a cent. The plan is to own wheat at any cent level just as long as wheat continues to break so it may be bought.

BUT! whenever any lot rallies to where it has a two cent profit, sell it. Place your order ahead so when the price is reached your trade is completed. Sometimes the market will immediately drop again, so place your order immediately to repurchase the lot sold out.

ANY LOT BOUGHT ON A SCALE DOWN WILL YIELD A PROFIT eventually and probably very soon. The use of a fixed plan such as this enables the operator to keep a neat set of books showing purchases, sales, profits, margin balance, and the number of lots awaiting sale. As soon as a lot is bought the broker should be given an order to sell it at its proper place. Take a carbon copy of all orders and keep them for reference until the order is filled. See that your broker does his part. Watch your margin fund and don't buy a single lot more than you can margin below all danger levels. For instance if you are buying wheat on a one or two cent scale down from 60, see that you have enough money to margin each lot 50% of its cost price. See page 34.

When followed in a business-like manner, wheat trading can be made a highly profitable profession and will amount to merchandising as certainly as if you were handling the actual grain. This is the highest type of wheat market practice and can be built into a business of mammoth proportions if the trader persists.

MAKE YOUR TRADING PAY NOW

There's no need for waiting until some grand climax happens in the wheat market, some vast damage to the crop, some war or some president's "bull wheat market." Sharp rallies or breaks are following rapidly one upon another and your studies of market action herein show you that you can always get into the trend on the correct side. That's the first requisite of success. Study KEY NUMBER THREE in Book II. If the market is in bear trend, catch wheat on the first rally and start your selling operations. Don't fear but what your option will decline. It's the law of the market.

TAKE YOUR PROFITS! Enough is enough. You can't make a fortune on one 5000 bushel trade, therefore, let it yield its little share and prepare to make another and another.

If you discover the market is in bull trend and is yet not far from bottom levels, buy on a scale down every one cent, if you can margin the lots, or every two cents down. If you can margin only one lot wait for one of those "vertical breaks" of five or more cents and buy. **Then stick to your trade** until it yields its profit. You remember how Jacob of old got into a terrible scrap with an angel one dark night. He wrestled with the angel until the peep of dawn when the angel had enough and wanted to call the match off. Jacob, however, had a "half Nelson" or a "scissor's hold" on his feathery adversary and refused to let go until the angel "blessed him."

Make your trade according to correct principles and it will surely bless you. You can spend valuable years of your life trying to make money by jumping in and out, first long, then short, like 90% of the traders do and each year have less money than you had at the start.

Set your face toward big things. Every man who has amassed a fortune had his small beginnings, but he was content to grow big slowly and steadily knowing fully the vast power of systematic personal effort and above all a knowledge of his business. How successful the reader of these lines will be depends on how much in earnest he is to make money in the wheat market. "Hidden fortunes" await the man who will follow the market according to its known laws.

"SOMETHING TO CONSIDER"

"I was born and brought up in Gloucester, Massachusetts, a seafaring city which teaches many things not learned from books and blackboards. When you are caught in rough water, with the wind blowing harder every minute and the waves rising higher, the situation often looks like sure disaster. But just as the mounting seas reach a critical height where it seems that one foot more will swamp you, those waves lengthen out; and instead of driving through them, you begin to ride over them. Those who study the ways of God and the teaching of history do not collapse in a crisis. They drive ahead as best they can, having faith that at the very moment when all seems lost — the waves will lengthen out!"

—Rober W. Babson.

BOOK SIX

Science and Secrets of the Wheat Market

A clear, brief course of study in market
action with practical instructions for
the profitable use of the grain market

In Six Books

By Burton Homer Pugh

Author of

A Better Way to Make Money in Wheats and Stocks
Traders Instruction Book
Mastering Cotton

LAMBERT-GANN PUBLISHING CO.
P. O. Box 0
Pomeroy, Washington 99347

PRINTED IN U S A

THE SUPREME EVENT IN WHEAT

The most thrilling event in the ceaseless activities of wheat is a strong bull movement. All other types of action fade into insignificance before this onrushing, boiling, resistless geyser of enthusiasm that sends the market up week after week to a towering top.

It is a homecoming, a get-together event for the wheat trading family of the world. It is once when they can all agree and travel along together—for awhile.

No matter how discordant the relations between bulls and bears may be during seventy-five per cent of the time when the price is drifting, the warring factions join hands in perfect fraternal amity when wheat gets into one of those determined advances which, for want of a better name, is termed A BULL MOVE-MENT.

Bounding prices proclaim a story of better times, of prosperous farms, of easier money and financial serenity ahead. To business they become a par-excellent stimulant and when it is a rising wheat market the effect is felt instantly in all of the earth's great nations. This brilliant type of movement is fortunately of simple origin. It runs its course to the end with power and with such delightful definiteness that even the enemies of the market submerge their animosities and join in with the jostling, jovial bull market crowd. The bull move is the wheat market at blossom time. It is the thankful approbation of the race in its happiest mood for its greatest food.

2

But a blossoming wheat market, like all other flowering phenomena must wither and die. The geyser spouts and subsides, the volcano erupts violently, then sinks into peaceful tranquility. These forces expend themselves and sink back to a normal level. Nothing does this more surely or quickly than an erupting wheat market and, since we have so many past examples of bull moves to inspect, it is comparatively easy to get at the causes of such moves, how they start, how they travel along and, most important of all, how they **make their finish.**

Nearly all bull movements start for a good reason. Nine out of ten such advances follow heavy crop damage which reduces the supply and stimulates the demand, but public enthusiasm carries prices up far beyond a normal price and a decline invariably ensues. Professional traders and other shrewd speculators capitalize this human habit of overdoing things by letting the amateur traders, who greatly predominate, run the market up to a high figure, then sell out to them. For some unaccountable reason men will place the maximum of investment in the market and give it the minimum of study. They have not the slightest knowledge of market action, how a bull movement starts, how it thrives, "blossoms" out into a fast, furious rise—then dies. The sole and ardent wish of the crowd is to be "in on something" that's good.

For awhile nearly everybody makes money in a bull movement. Jones hears how Brown, his neighbor, made a fine haul in the market. The secretary hears how his boss made a thousand or two. At the club it is quickly noised about that several "lucky dogs" have big paper profits in wheat, and the rush to the market grows, but unfortunately it takes so long for the skeptical public to become convinced that the advance in wheat is well along before the heavy buying comes in. It is this last feverish stage of buying that tells the experienced speculator the end is near. When he hears that clerks, bell boys, stenographers, bootblacks and cab drivers are buying wheat **he sells out!**

SHORT MEMORIES

The memory of traders is short. Talk to a score of traders and you will find perhaps one who has some idea of how or why a bull move starts, but few are those who understand how to follow it through to the end. Yet these bull markets have been happening right along with singular frequency. Nine of them occurred since November, 1924, to November 9, 1931. They all have practically the same ear-marks, follow the same general habits on the way up, and all of them top out with the same grand, upward rush, yet all of these common habits are forgotten from one bull move to another, and the next such move finds the mass of the public as ignorant of market action as it was for all the years past.

Now there is not a single extenuating excuse for an intelligent person, able to read the English language and who will chart the simple movements of a wheat option, to make the blunders of the "crowd." A certain percentage of traders grow immensely wealthy by making a close study of these simple wheat movements and by following methods which the lazy minded masses will not take time to find out. Any institution—like the market—which is made by men can be understood by men. Market movements are not an enigma, a joke or a farce. They are the natural efforts of the people to adjust prices to fit the demand.

The reader of these pages has the power to acquire unforgetable methods of forecasting a bull movement in wheat and of following it through to its conclusion at a highly gratifying profit. Of all market demonstrations the bull market is the most direct and profitable. It pays to learn bull market habits with the same thoroughness that the surgeon comes to know the use of his tools. Large operators who trade in millions of bushels—sometimes ten to twenty millions—will wait patiently for a year or more for the proper conditions to arise that will support a bull movement. Their plan is to wait for bullish conditions with the price low. Then they strike and strike hard. At the top when everybody is bullish they sell out. This is why, as we have told you, that bull markets are started and stopped by professional traders.

4

EARLY BULL MARKET SYMPTOMS

You have doubtless watched several bull movements getting under way during past years without realizing that those dull days were maturing days when the market was surreptitiously making a very definite turn.

All bull markets start from low prices, so the observer should be on the watch whenever he finds the market acting dull at low prices and especially if the price is down near the low levels of the **previous bear wheat market.**

Some years the market will make many moderate swings before it finally gets away for its big move. The conditions are not quite right. More crop damage must occur. Therefore, not every swing bottom is the foundation for a bull move.

The trader who is waiting patiently for a bull move may make several trades—and profitable ones—before the real movement develops. If the moon phase conditions are right with the full moon at the bottom of a swing and the price at the bottom of a vertical break, he can buy, and, when the move is well in his favor, place an **open stop** slightly above where he got it and "go off and leave it." If the bull move starts, he's in. If it proves to be just another swing, he goes out at his stop without loss.

Watch the crop conditions with one eye and the quotation board with the other. The board will reflect the correct crop condition better than the crop reporters. Often an advance will occur after what appears to be a bearish report or break after a bullish report. Every man who trades is a crop reporter for his community. He trades according to how wheat looks in his locality. This local trading is felt every day while the crop reports come monthly. That's why it is so often said that the market has already "discounted" the report.

SPEED IS CHARM—IN THE WHEAT MARKET

Everybody wants the market to start right out in a gallop as soon as he gets in. He is even peeved a little if it does not get into action in the way he thinks it ought to. But there are a lot of traders in an active wheat market, perhaps ten thousand trades take place in a day during a big market, and it takes considerable time for the bunch to change over to one opinion or the other.

The bull wheat market is highly desirable because it runs a long way and runs fast. It satisfies that human desire to make a lot of money in a hurry. Whether quick money stays with us or not, it is sought as eagerly now as it was a hundred or a thousand years ago.

One of the fastest wheat markets the author has ever witnessed occurred in 1922, some ten years ago, following a dry winter and a series of dust storms in January and February that promised to shave off the top crust of the southwestern wheat states and take the crop with it. "Crop killed in three states" was one statement in the wire news, and those who looked up into the dust laden heavens thought it was true, but while much wheat was damaged during the windy weather, rains starting by March brought the crop out to a yield of 867,000,000, or nearly as much as we had in our great depression year of surplus 1932.

This 1922 bull move is charted for your inspection on page 7. It is beautifully regular in all of its features, having started according to the usual plan noted in KEY NO. 1, Book II, and followed the moon phases right on through to the top, where it yields gracefully to the Minor Trend line and begins its long decline. A crop scare was entirely responsible for the move, but from start to finish our student could trade and follow its steps and was enabled, far ahead, to pick the time when the market would make top. He might not have been able to estimate the top figure, but he could tell the time by the new moon phase, which is as good or better. The move started from 107½ and rose to 149⅞. It was a six weeks bull move which more properly started with the NEW MOON PHASE of January 13, 1922.

6

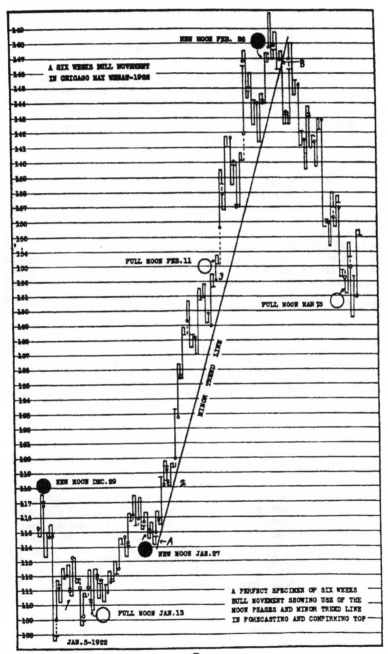

A SIX WEEKS BULL MOVEMENT
IN CHICAGO MAY WHEAT-1922

NEW MOON FEB. 26

FULL MOON FEB.11

FULL MOON MAR 13

MINOR TREND LINE

NEW MOON DEC.29

NEW MOON JAN.27

A PERFECT SPECIMEN OF SIX WEEKS
BULL MOVEMENT SHOWING USE OF THE
MOON PHASES AND MINOR TREND LINE
IN FORECASTING AND CONFIRMING TOP

FULL MOON JAN.13

JAN.3-1922

7

A CRYSTAL CLEAR MOVEMENT

While the reader has seen many excellent graphs of bull movements in the previous books of this course he will find that none of them exceed the one charted on page 7. It is a very excellent example of a six-weeks bull movement, running true to form with the moon phases and snugly bounded by the minor trend line for almost the entire extent of the advance.

It will be noted that following the new moon phase of December 29, 1921, there was a sharp break of ten cents. This vertical break immediately placed the market in an excellent position for "accumulation" by professional traders. They well know that such a break clears out the longs, loads the market with a heavy short interest and leaves the price practically certain to advance. Ten days elapsed before the professionals secured their desired load of wheat, but by January 13, as noted on the chart, wheat was ready to go up. It advanced seven cents in as many days. This was the first or slow stage of this particular bull movement. Sometimes the slow stage covers a full month or two phases of the moon.

This brilliant movement made all of its preparations from January 3 to January 27. From then on for a full month the price rushed upward, stimulated by sensational news from the wheat states, where the wind was blowing the crop out, apparently by whole counties.

There was only one way to forecast the end of this advance, the NEW MOON DATE OF FEBRUARY 26, which is noted at the top of the chart.

Our student trader, seeing this advance getting under way, could easily have diagnosed it as a bull movement and seeing that it started properly at the full moon phase of January 13 he would immediately have concluded that the movement would make top around February 26, six weeks later on the NEW MOON DATE, regardless of the price level. That is, he could have told when the top would occur but not where.

8

TO KNOW WHEN a bull movement will make top is almost as desirable as to know the actual top figures. The trader can take his time, can hold his peace and wait for the movement to run its course. The author knows of no sure way to estimate the top of a six weeks bull movement except by a knowledge of the moon phases and how they mark the stages of the movement. This is the shortest type of bull movement and is also the most frequent. Since January, 1922, eleven bull movements have occurred in wheat, eight of which have been of the six weeks type. The others ran three months, four months and seven months.

The great usefulness of the minor trend line is well illustrated in this movement. The trader, in charting this action from its beginning, is not sure a minor trend line can be used until the straight upward advance after the new moon January 27. He immediately draws this line, starting at A and placing it against the first important reaction (four lines above A). This line holds through to the finish and at B furnishes confirmation of the downtrend, where the market breaks sharply below the line.

Now in this movement, as in nearly all other bull movements, the trader has the welcome advantage of three powerful market indicators, viz.:

THE MOON PHASES which point out the top.
THE RETURN MOVEMENT which follows the vertical rise.
THE MINOR TREND LINE which shows start of downtrend.

It requires a little patience and a little faith at the start of such a movement, to convince one's self that a big advance is in the making because the three weeks from January 3 to January 27 finds the news full of confusing reports and the bearish element advising short sales as always happens at the bottom of declines. The safest way is to let the charted action of your option furnish its own indications. It faithfully reflects the majority opinion. Give only passing attention to the news, but watch the action of each day intently.

9

GETTING THE MONEY

THE VERY NEXT BULL MOVEMENT which the trader sees will doubtless be similar to the one charted on page 7. He may be waiting for it with full intentions to get in, or it may be in progress as he reads this book.

The unqualified desire is to get in as near the bottom as possible, follow it through to the top and SELL OUT THERE!

Let's run through this 1922 bull move just as though it were in progress at the time you are reading these lines.
FIRST, you buy on the January 3 break because you know the return movement will carry the price back up to at least 115. As yet you may not suspect a bull movement is in the making.

SECOND, you find the full moon phase is ushered in on January 13 and that it starts the price upward rapidly. Then you begin to think a big move possible and take special note of the next new moon phase to see how the market acts. When the price goes on above the new moon date level you discover it is moving rapidly and have practical confirmation thereby that a bull move is under progress.

You have presumably bought one lot at 110.
Now you buy another lot on a reaction at 2.

You draw a minor trend line under the market as shown at A-B and watch the market climb. You buy another lot, the third one around 3, because you know the market has another two weeks to go and that it will make top on the new moon date or near it.

Finally you sell out on the February 26 phase, or when the market breaks below the minor trend line as at B. In following the market according to these plans you perform the rare feat of buying into a big advance at the bottom and selling out at the top. It is naturally a little more difficult than it appears from reading this, but observation and practice will develop your skill.

THE BEAR MARKET

Now we come to that type of movement which is diametrically opposite to the bull movement. When the market makes a top and turns downward an entirely new set of forces comes into play. Incidentally a different type of human emotions enters the market. From the buoyant, optimistic, heedless belief in higher prices the majority of traders seem to suddenly develop a pessimistic attitude, an opposition to the advance. Experience has taught shrewd operators that mass opinion causes movements to overrun in either direction and that a market is especially susceptible to a decline after one of those over-extended tops.

Therefore, after a bull market has made top the sensible trader immediately reverses his position, curbs his bullish ideas and adjusts himself to the long decline which invariably follows the bull movement.

One of the best qualifications for the successful trader is the ability to reverse with the big turns in the market and to follow the trend in either direction until it is exhausted.

The moon may be disregarded after the first break from the top. It is a perfectly clear matter that the moon should not exert much force in a bear market, because declines are brought about by the operations of a very small minority of traders. The public is ninety per cent bullish as a mass and when the bull movement is over, most of them quit and the small number left operating on the bear side are not sufficient to produce moon phase effects. Therefore, the skillful trader will adjust himself to the downtrend for the next several months, using the Multi-Profit Plan, as described heretofore.

The student trader should be impressed with the extreme usefulness of the moon phases in the six weeks bull market and those occasional swings which catch the market on a high swing during a new moon phase or at the bottom of a vertical break. Outside of these the moon phases may be more safely ignored.

11

All through this book the bull movement and the bear movement must be discussed side by side. One is dependent upon the other. One exists because of the other. While they work opposite to each other, yet one is born as the other dies.

Most bull markets run their course rapidly while all bear markets drag down slowly, using much more time for the reason that a bear market is going against public feeling, which always prefers higher prices.

The above paragraph explains why some operators become attached to the short side. They find that bearish operations can continue much longer than bullish operations. The bull movement runs so fast as to confuse them while the bear market works in a slower fashion and is more to their liking.

THE BEAR MARKET LAW is very simple:
A RETARDED MOVEMENT OF PRICES FROM ABOVE NORMAL TO BELOW NORMAL.

Every one of the bull markets charted in this set of books was followed by a bear market that ran much longer than the bull market. While it may take a bull movement only six weeks to run up to a complete top, it will take from four to six months for the price to get back down to where it started. When the **economic trend** is downward the successive bear market will go lower than the previous ones.

Bull markets advance by two stages. The first or slow stage and the rapid or finishing stage. Bear markets break by two stages, first the rapid stage and second the long, slow stage. Thus it is observed that the action of a bear market is exactly opposite to a bull market in both stages. As the student goes through these charted movements he will discover the amazing simplicity of these two greatest movements in wheat and how they may be followed with the most gratifying success.

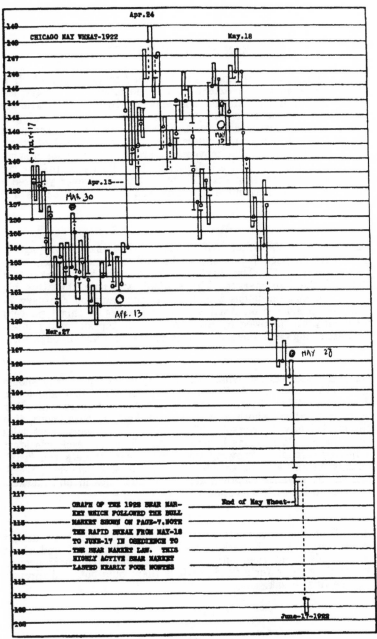

Apr.24

CHICAGO MAY WHEAT-1922

May.18

MAY.17

Apr.15---

MAR 30

Apr.15---

Mar.27

Apr. 13

MAY 25

MAY 28

GRAPH OF THE 1922 BEAR MAR-
KET WHICH FOLLOWED THE BULL
MARKET SHOWN ON PAGE-7. NOTE
THE RAPID BREAK FROM MAY-18
TO JUNE-17 IN OBEDIENCE TO
THE BEAR MARKET LOW. THIS
HIGHLY ACTIVE BEAR MARKET
LASTED NEARLY FOUR MONTHS

End of May Wheat--

June-17-1922

13

BEAR MARKET HABITS

On a previous page we gave you the bear market law, which is quite simple as to the extent of the move, but the longer the market delays in finishing its bear movement the more erratic are its swings. As we have told you in a previous book, the biggest swings are found in bear markets. This is because a bull movement invites a large number of traders into the market, most of whom make money during the movement, and they continue playing actively for months after a bull market top. This accounts for the huge volume of trading that follows a top. Wherever you see a bear market in this course of study you will find it active and erratic.

On page 13 is the other half of the market charted on page 7. The chart on page 7 is a six weeks bull movement which made top on February 27. The chart on page 13 is the bear market that followed the bull market. The student will note that this big movement made a double top, the first top being on February 27 and the second top on April 24. Big advances of this type very frequently are followed by a perfect double top and many inter-mediate swings and movements such as are observed on page 13.

Naturally you will ask what caused the double top or why should the market undergo the three weeks congestion just above the date March 27? That is because professional traders and other large speculators, who have access to brokerage house books, find the market heavily oversold. That is, they find heavy short sales with inadequate margins behind them. These professionals start a buying campaign, knowing that these short traders will "run" quickly on any sign of an advance. It was short covering which caused the advance on April 15. All double tops in bull markets are caused by such operations.

But all of the movements charted on page 13 are bear market movements. The bull market was over on February 27 and wheat was a sale from then on. Even those who sold short around March 27 were in for a good profit if they could but hold through for the final break.

The charted movement on page 13 would readily confuse any trader unacquainted with market laws, but to the student of this course it should be an open book. He knows that once a bull market top has been made he can reverse his trading plan and sell short on all rallies either in a single lot or on a two-cent scale up, preferably the latter.

Immense profits are available in active markets such as you are now studying. Follow the bull market to its conclusion first of all, then reverse and stay with the bear side until the price is back down to approximately where it started. THEN ABANDON THE SHORT SIDE!

This procedure is simple but it is eminently correct. Prices of wheat are forever running from a bull market to a bear market and back again. There are only two basic trends in wheat, the upward trend, which breeds bull movements, and the downtrend, which breeds bear markets.

A thorough comprehension of the bull market and the bear market lets the trader into all of the worth while secrets of market action.

It will seem to be a platitude to the student, but the only barrier to success when you follow these natural laws of the market is in your own weakness. If you can lay down an inviolable rule for yourself and keep it that you will not make a trade unless it has a heavy margin to protect it, you can take almost unlimited rewards from the wheat market.

HIDDEN FORTUNES IN WHEAT are not deeply hidden. Market action is surprisingly simple. That you have discovered in the laws of the market studied herein. Govern your eagerness to make money, protect your earned profits by not overtrading and keep adding to your capital so your deals may be larger and eventually you will find yourself in a financial class which you had thought you could never attain.

BEAR MARKET POINTERS

The bear market is more definite than the bull market.

The top of a bull market must be estimated and may vary considerably from prices forecast, but a bear market has a definite, measured distance to decline.

A second top may exceed the first top in a bull market, but it does not prevent the bear market from running to its full decline.

On page 13 it will be noted that regardless of the three months delay in starting down the bear market made its way to bottom with amazing certainty.

The Multi-Profit Plan applied to the short side in this big market would have resulted in astonishing profits and not a single loss.

A bull market runs its course rapidly with comparatively few reactions. The bear market takes more time and undergoes many sharp reactions.

Many traders make handsome profits in a bull movement and lose them in the following bear market because they keep trying to play the bull side on a declining market.

The choicest knowledge for grain men and speculators is to know the trend. There are but two important trends, the upward or bull market trend and the downward or bear market trend. Once these two are thoroughly understood success should be easy. The economic trend may be ignored.

"In and out traders" should acquaint themselves thoroughly with vertical rises and vertical breaks, with the minor trend line and the other lesser means of detecting swings, but the long pull operator should follow the trend only.

From the time a bull market makes top until the price is back down to the bottom again usually covers from three to six months.

When a bear market is down to where the bull market started or near there, then the operator should abandon the bear side and follow the bull side only, buying on reactions and selling on rallies until the next bull market is completed.

16

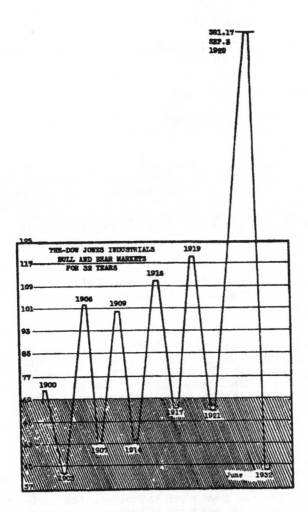

THE LAW OF BULL AND BEAR MARKETS as applied to stocks.
The top figures are the tops of bull movements. The lower figures
are the bottoms of bear markets. Whether the bull move be small
as in 1900 or far up as in 1929, the average price comes back down
to the narrow limits of 42 to 65 shown in the shaded zone. Whether
it be wheat or U. S. Steel, the laws of market action are the same.

17

THE BULL MARKET LAW:

A RAPID RISE OF PRICES FROM BELOW NORMAL
TO ABOVE NORMAL.

THE BEAR MARKET LAW:

A RETARDED MOVEMENT OF PRICES FROM ABOVE
NORMAL TO BELOW NORMAL.

By the momentum of enthusiasm a bull market is carried far too
high. By unreasoning pessimism a bear market is carried too low.
The result of these two psychological impulses that drive a market
first too high then too low is to form the basis for the **Law of
Action and Reaction** so often quoted in Mr. Babson's works.
ACTION AND REACTION ARE EQUAL BUT IN OPPOSITE
DIRECTIONS.

The return movement, described in Book IV of this set, is an application of this simple law to the smaller events in the market such
as sharp swings.

In order to show the simple definiteness of bull and bear market
laws a graph of the Dow-Jones industrials for 32 years back is
shown on page 17. The low prices shown in the shaded zone are
evidently considered below normal by the mass opinion of our
people because each time prices drop down into that zone, buying
in heavy volume develops.

There is no way to tell how high the stock market may be carried
by bullish enthusiasm, but it may be depended upon to come back
down to the shaded zone. Every one of the bull movements shown
was followed by a bear market which carried prices **approximately**
down to the level from which the previous bull market started.
From 1903 to 1906 was a big bull market period in stocks. Yet
before the end of 1907 the price was down nearly to where it
started in 1903.

Were it convenient to chart the price movements of cattle, hogs,
real estate or any security or commodity in which public masses
deal, it would be found that they are incessantly performing according to the above simple market laws.

MARKET LORE IS GOLDEN

In all of the market movements of wheat the bull market stands out like a lighthouse. Its sequel is the bear market. A complete knowledge of these two great movements is a potential fortune to the ambitious wheat trader. The market places no limitations on the man who is clever enough to know its habits and follow its moods. "With all thy getting get knowledge," said the crafty old proverb writer of 3,000 years ago, who not only wrote the best philosophy in the best language of the ancients but was able to "collect" enough money to build a seventy-seven million dollar temple to commemorate his financial ability.

Several lesser means of indicating market movements have been carefully placed before the student in these books and while they are of great importance they will be found to serve as accessories to the two great events of the wheat market, the bull movement and the bear movement. Whether the student acquires a taste for the short in and out trades or plays for the big movements, he will find his most cherished information will be what he knows about the trend.

Getting down to **gold tacks,** the trader who studies the laws and habits of the wheat market, as the reader is doing now, has an open road to wealth. The big profit making movements are simple and clear to anyone who wants to know them. They run true to form, and will continue to do so because they are grounded in human nature. Small movements excite small traders and muddle their opinions. Those who fail must lay the fault at their own feet because the market has its laws and obeys them. The individual must know what the market is doing, must work with the trend, not ignore it. Key days, time cycles, stop loss orders, averages or other schemes used to **trick the market** will only trick the user. But the trader who will use a 50% margin on every lot traded in, will take not less than a two or three cent per bushel profit on every lot and will trade in harmony with the trend is headed for the goal of financial success.

19

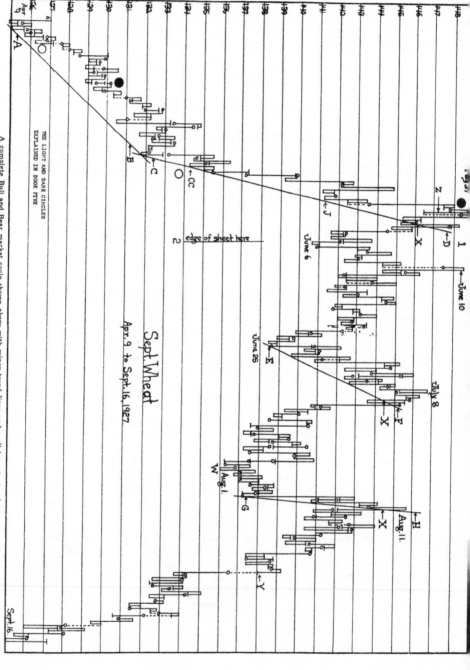

Sept. Wheat
Apr. 9 to Sept. 16, 1927

THE LIGHT AND DARK CIRCLES
EXPLAINED IN BOOK FIVE

A complete Bull and Bear market cycle shown above with minor trend lines under all important swings.

MARKET SUCCESS—FINANCIAL SUCCESS

To acquire financial success you must follow the laws that govern acquisition. They are few but imperative. Substitutes will not work. Success in market operations is the same. It can be accomplished only by observing and using the laws of action by which the market is governed. Fortunately market laws are simple. The chief mistakes of the individual are in confusing his personal habits with market laws. He says petulantly, "I'm always wrong. When I buy, it goes down, and when I sell, it goes up." He thinks the market is forever being manipulated against the small trader. If he were aware of the genuine laws of market action he would know that regardless of temporary manipulations, which do exist in the market, the movements run their courses in obedience to inescapable laws which are not mysterious or difficult.

Take the graph on pages 20-21. If the reader had been watching this market at the time he would have been sure a bull movement was in progress by the time prices had reached the level B or C and could have bought for a big advance. He would have been following a true market law, and could have sold out with a handsome reward around top figures by the means taught in this course. THEN HE COULD REVERSE and sell wheat for a full decline to the starting point and take another enormous profit. His returns would exceed anything possible to accomplish otherwise, because he would be using the two premier movements of the market.

These laws are facts, not accidents. They are the tools for your success. There is no need of trying to trick the market out of meager, reluctant profits when you can use it according to its favorite laws and draws from its abundance. The difference between success and failure is expressed in the single word knowleage. Every sincere person is entitled to the good things of life, but Dame Fortune favors those who walk hand in hand with her simple homely laws. Success is the great event of life. Time is precious. Avoid the frivolities so common to small traders and lay your plans to get the best rewards the market has to offer.

PROOFS PILE UP

To the earnest student of market action confirming proofs multiply. The different styles of action fall into line with the two main trends and unite to confirm market laws. The small unessential movements quickly show their frailty and merge into the more stately movements. Confidence is born in the mind of the trader and he lays sound financial plans.

Graphs of other movements used in other books of this course can now be viewed with a new interest. On page 23 of Book II is a six weeks bull movement which ran its course perfectly according to the moon phases and topped out on the correct phase. The minor trend line (not shown here) confirmed the decline.

On page 11, Book II, is a bull movement in rye of the six weeks type running true to form in up and down trends.

On page 10, Book II, is a small sized bull and bear market in corn. The vertical rise of the bull move and the complete return, to starting point, of the bear movement is pictured with great clearness. Moon phases not used in corn.

On page 13, Book III, is another bull movement in corn. The complete return of the price to starting point was made but does not show on the graph.

On page 7, Book IV, is a complete bull and bear movement in oats. It runs true to form in every feature.

On page 18, Book II, is an extended bull movement followed by a perfect return of the bear movement.

On page 34, Book IV, will be seen the tempestuous bull market in which the battle of big operators occurred. The bear market made its usual complete return to the starting level.

Other charted markets to follow this page will further confirm these two most powerful movements and show the student trader what makes trend and how to follow it.

A STEP HIGHER

Every new thing the market student learns takes him a step higher on the ladder of success. It should be a matter of consolation that the chief laws motivating the market are few and are not intricate. They can be mastered while the trader is operating. "Practice makes perfect," runs the old copybook phrase and for the trader it has a deep truth for only by constantly charting, studying and trading can he come into the full, profitable knowledge of wheat market action. So amazingly remunerative is wheat that the trader can afford to take unlimited pains to learn its market phenomena. It will pay in proportion to how well one understands its deep laws. The small movements which ensnare tens of thousands of men must be ignored as fatal to success. Small daily activities are but tiny fractions of a big movement. The sun rises and sets every day but it takes months to make a season. Famous traders whose operations have made them of national reputation, play for large movements only.

Another highly useful piece of bull market information is shown the student on the following page in which he will see a graph of the biggest bull wheat market since the war period, that of 1924-1925, when wheat advanced a full dollar per bushel from the extreme low.

Extended bull markets that run several months obey, only partially, the influence of the moon phases; hence it is necessary to estimate the top through other means. A "top rule for extended bull movements" was dug out of market action several years ago by the author and is now passed on to the student to help complete his repertorie of market knowledge. This rule is strange almost to the extent of being without explanation. The early beginnings of an extended bull movement are no different than those of the six weeks type but the uptrend makes its way slowly running through several moon phases without developing fast action. The trader would be at a loss to know what to expect if he were not aware of the action of the slow bull movement. This is described in the pages which follow and is highly useful information enabling the trader to play for extraordinary profits. Out of eleven bull movements during the last ten years three have been of the long slow type.

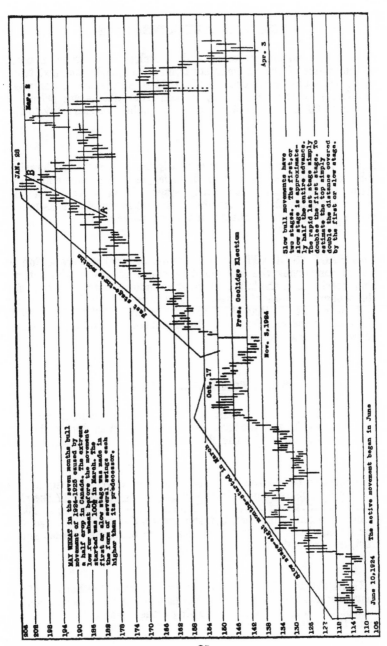

TIDAL MARKET MOVEMENTS

Heavy mass movements occasionally develop in the wheat market as the result of almost complete bullish persuasion amongst traders. Such a movement occurred in 1924-25 and is charted on page 25. The price of wheat having broken from $3.50—war price—to around $1.00 in early 1924 converted the public unreservedly to the bull side.

Heavy movements proceed more slowly but are well nigh irresistable. Short sellers are few in these larger movements which explains the slowness of the early stage. Short sellers in a bull movement cause the fast, finishing advance in the six weeks movements but are almost absent in the big movements.

THE PAGE 25 CHART omits a number of smaller days action to permit condensing the movement on one page. All of the natural characteristics of the bull movement are shown and will be easy for the thoughtful student to follow. The most notable feature of big bull movements is that they do not run their full route between three moon phases. Tops must be estimated by another method as shown in the rule below.

RULE FOR BULL MOVEMENTS

To estimate the distant top of a slowly advancing bull movement, wait for fast action to begin, then double the advance covered by the slow stage.

Use chart on page 25 as example. The slow movement began back in March. The extreme bottom was 100½. By October 17 the slow stage had advanced to 152½. Then came the slow decline to 138½ which was not liquidation but the preparation of a big movement for its last half. No way to estimate top until the market shows fast, upward action.

THE FIRST HALF is the advance covered from the bottom of the last bear market to the top of the last swing prior to fast action. The bottom was 100½, the last swing made top at 152½; therefore, note the method in figures.

First half or slow stage from 100½ to 152½—52 cents.
To estimate top, double the movement. 152½ plus 52 cents
The result is 204½. The actual top January 28 was 205⅞.

The above method is simple and, studied along with the chart, can be quickly mastered. It applies to all big tidal bull movements such as the advance in stocks from 1921 to 1929 and the bull movement of U. S. Steel from 1928 to 1929.

Another slow bull wheat movement is shown on page 18 of Book II of this set. It is the slow movement of wheat in 1928. The previous bottom to this advance was at 121½ in December 1927. Using the "Rule for slow bull movements," the bull market top is estimated as follows:

First half or slow stage from 121½ to 145—23½
To estimate top, double the movement. 145 plus 23½
The result is 168½. The actual top April 30 was 171¼.

It will be noted that the **fast rise** began from 145 up. It is not an exact rule but is the best means known of forecasting the top of a long drawn-out bull market. In the six weeks bull movements the moon phases may be relied upon as the best indication possible. These longer movements fail to keep step with the phases all the way up, hence it is necessary to use the **Bull market rule.**

Just why the last rapid rise in a bull movement should go as far as the first slow stage is a problem of psychology, but it is so profound a habit that other examples may be adduced as a matter of confirmation. Charts will be seen on page 28 of two huge, slow bull movements in the stock market, the largest known to speculative history. Study the Bull Market Rule carefully for conditions following the 1931-1932 depression will foster a big advance in wheat. If the movement gets off rapidly use the moon phases to forecast the top. If the movement makes slow headway, use the Bull Market Rule.

27

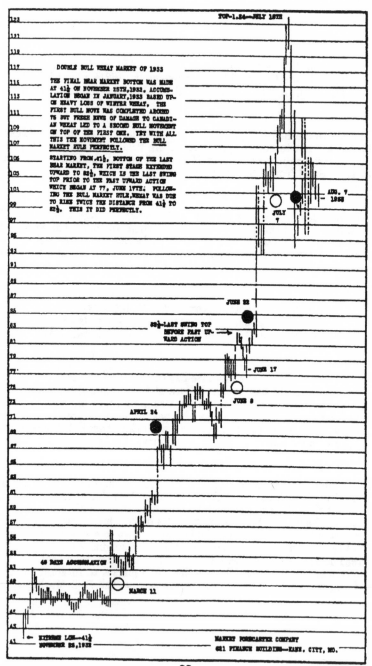

DOUBLE BULL WHEAT MARKET OF 1933

THE FINAL BEAR MARKET BOTTOM WAS MADE
AT 41½ ON NOVEMBER 25TH, 1932. ACCUMU-
LATION BEGAN IN JANUARY, 1933 BASED UP-
ON HEAVY LOSS OF WINTER WHEAT. THE
FIRST BULL MOVE WAS COMPLETED AROUND
76 BUT FRESH NEWS OF DAMAGE TO CANADI-
AN WHEAT LED TO A SECOND BULL MOVEMENT
ON TOP OF THE FIRST ONE. YET WITH ALL
THIS THE MOVEMENT FOLLOWED THE BULL
MARKET RULE PERFECTLY.

STARTING FROM 41½, BOTTOM OF THE LAST
BEAR MARKET, THE FIRST STAGE EXTENDED
UPWARD TO 83½, WHICH IS THE LAST SWING
TOP PRIOR TO THE FAST UPWARD ACTION
WHICH BEGAN AT 77, JUNE 17TH; FOLLOW-
ING THE BULL MARKET RULE, WHEAT WAS DUE
TO RISE TWICE THE DISTANCE FROM 41½ TO
83½. THIS IT DID PERFECTLY.

TOP—1.24—JULY 18TH

AUG. 7
1933

JULY
7

JUNE 22

83½—LAST SWING TOP
BEFORE FAST UP-
WARD ACTION

JUNE 17

JUNE 8

APRIL 24

40 DAYS ACCUMULATION

MARCH 11

← EXTREME LOW—41½
NOVEMBER 25, 1932

MARKET FORECASTER COMPANY
621 FINANCE BUILDING—KANS. CITY, MO.

28

THE BULL MARKET RULE

The Bull Market Rule, as described on page 26 is shown with remarkable fidelity in the last big bull movement which culminated on the 18th of July, 1933. This book was held back from the printer long enough to enable me to insert a chart of this excellent bull move with a description of the BULL MARKET RULE and how it applies.

This "rule" is a discovery original with the writer and is one of the most useful rules known to market science.

The bottom of the wheat market—during the depression—was made November 25 at 41½.

The next bull market began at once but so slowly that few people suspected it was beginning.

From January to March a narrow accumulative market developed which became more aggressive in March after the "bank holiday". The advance set in powerfully in March, therefore, the **Full Moon** date being in the midst of the Bank holiday. The "six weeks" advance from March 11 to April 24 appeared to be a finished bull movement but a further advance to the 75 level showed bullish sentiment increasing. The exciting cause was the danger to the Canadian wheat crop from dry weather.

THE LAST SWING TOP at 82½ (December Wheat) was followed by **fast action** beginning on June 17. The Full Moon date governing this last rapid "six weeks" movement was on June 18 as shown. From then on to the final top at 124 the advance developed into a wild affair, yet with all this boiling enthusiasm the top finished at almost the exact level forecasted by the **Bull Market Rule.** Note the rule on page 26.

The advantage of this rule is as follows:
> During the first or slow stage the trader can maintain a long position confidently or can pyramid on a scale up knowing that the advance will not be **half** through until **fast action begins** (as June 17).

When the last (fast action) stage sets in the trader can buy additional lots with confidence for a big advance and can estimate the final top.

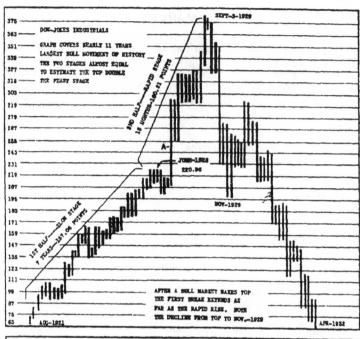

DOW-JONES INDUSTRIALS

GRAPH COVERS NEARLY 11 YEARS
LARGEST BULL MOVEMENT OF HISTORY
THE TWO STAGES ALMOST EQUAL
TO ESTIMATE THE TOP DOUBLE
THE FIRST STAGE

2ND HALF----RAPID STAGE
18 MONTHS-160.81 POINTS

SEPT-3-1929

A-

JUNE-1928
220.96

1ST HALF----SLOW STAGE
7 YEARS--157.06 POINTS

NOV-1929

AFTER A BULL MARKET MAKES TOP
THE FIRST BREAK EXTENDS AS
FAR AS THE RAPID RISE. NOTE
THE DECLINE FROM TOP TO NOV,-1929

AUG-1921

APR-1932

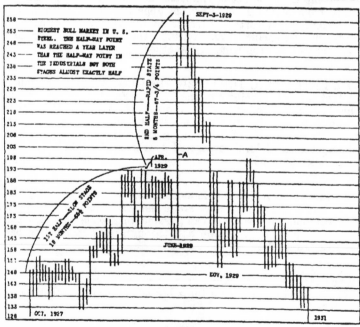

BIGGEST BULL MARKET IN U. S.
STEEL. THE HALF-WAY POINT
WAS REACHED A YEAR LATER
THAN THE HALF-WAY POINT IN
THE INDUSTRIALS BUT BOTH
STAGES ALMOST EXACTLY HALF

2ND HALF----RAPID STATE
6 MONTHS--67-3/4 POINTS

SEPT-3-1929

APR.
1929

-A

1ST HALF----SLOW STAGE
18 MONTHS--68 POINTS

JUNE-1929

NOV, 1929

OCT. 1927

1931

30

BIGGEST BULL MOVEMENT IN HISTORY

The bull stock market of 1921 to 1929 exceeded by three times the largest advance previously known to New York stocks. The graph on page 28 is shown to prove the validity of the author's "Bull Market Rule" for slow movements as given on page 26. This strange habit of a movement running half its expected advance, then doubling the distance in a fast, finishing rise is applicable only to the long time, long distance bull movements.

It will be noted that the Dow-Jones Industrials spent seven years working up to the point shown at June, 1928. Two or three months churning occurred here, followed by a very moderate break, then the sharp advance marked A.

The student trader, having studied the general habits of bull movements in this course, would know the advance was not finished at the top made in June, 1928 (220.96), because there had been no fast, top making action. He knows a further advance is due. He cannot confirm 220.96 as the finish of the first half until he sees the fast rise getting started. Immediately thereafter he is able to estimate the top with an accuracy that would amaze the wisest operators of Wall Street. Taking his pencil he would estimate the top as follows:

```
Level reached June, 1928  .................  220.96
Bottom of last bear market.................... 63.90
                                             -------
Distance covered by slow stage................157.06
Now to the first stage.................220.96
Add the difference....................157.06
                                             -------
Estimated top ..         ........378.02
```

The actual top was 381.17. Thus it is seen that regardless of the extent and violence of this enormous bull movement that it ran true to form with astonishing accuracy. The value of this information to stock operators, banks and trust companies at the time of the movement would be almost beyond computation. However, this discovery is original with the author and is now being published for the first time.

The two stages are naturally not exactly equal. A reasonable variation must be expected. As the student examines these great movements, the largest known to our speculative markets, he will marvel at the accuracy of this Bull Market Rule for slow bull movements. It places him in possession of knowledge that, in a single big movement, would enable him to make a comfortable fortune.

Every graph in this course is drawn from actual movements of the market. They are genuine and prove themselves. The aim of the author is to show the trader how to see and understand these market laws for himself, so he can profit by them. Ignorance of market action is expensive. Scores of other examples might be charted and described in these pages, but the laws taught herein run the same through all of them. The reader has the best examples of market action the market has to offer, and when he masters these books he should have a knowledge of the market equal to our nationally known professional traders.

The unprecedented depression of 1931-1932 brings investors into more studious market habits. Success is the all important aim, and since it could not be acquired by past careless methods men are seeking more adequate market knowledge. The enormous profit to be obtained when trading is done correctly cannot be sacrificed to easy going ignorance of market laws.

Fortunately for the trader, the market is easily understood when he grasps the few fundamental types of movement. It is not like a deep science that takes years of study. He can learn as he earns. He can start trading and acquire experience as he studies these lessons. Always it will be found that the most difficult task will be to keep one's individual greed controlled or to keep his ambitions for wealth within reasonable bounds. The lure of profits is strong in all of us, but is not unconquerable; remember what the "late" King Solomon said about the fellow who "ruleth his spirit."

U. S. STEEL, THE PATRIARCH OF STOCKS

To further confirm the Bull Market Rule your attention is invited
to the biggest bull movement in the leader of the stock market,
U. S. Steel. This movement was contemporary with the huge, eight
year bull market in stocks. Though it started about six years later
than the Dow-Jones Industrials, this stock made top at the same
time and declined with the other stocks.

The bull movement in Steel was naturally much shorter in duration
than the 30 Industrials. During the eight years of the industrial
advance hundreds of stocks had their bull movements and sank
back. It was the extended and combined bull movements in aggregate that made this huge stock market movement. U. S. Steel,
being a fragment of the market, naturally ran its course in a short
time.

Starting from the bottom or last bear market of U. S. Steel at
128½ in October, 1927, the advance made way rather slowly until
April, 1928, where a period of rapid oscillations occurred, but each
rally made top not far from the 193½ level. This halting period
covered two or three weeks. Then came the usual reaction that
precedes the final advance and the price dropped down to 164 about
June 1, 1929. From that bottom began the swiftest rise ever known
to this stock. Its rapid action at once proclaimed the fact that the
finishing or rapid stage was at hand. Our student knowing the bull
market rule would immediately be able to estimate the top with
commendable accuracy. Here is the way he would figure it out:

Level reached April, 1929		194
Bottom of last bear market		128½
Distance covered by slow stage		65½
Now to the first stage	194	
Add the difference	65½	
Estimated top		259½

The actual top reached was 261¾. Thus the accuracy of the rule
is again demonstrated. The top of the last swing prior to fast
action is the half way point of a big bull movement.

Other movements of both stocks and grains will occur in the future. At the moment you are reading this, wheat may be shaping itself into a movement that can be followed with immense profit, but no trader has the master hand until he knows the laws of market action. The reason for showing the graph of U. S. Steel is to prove by another of the market's chief members that these laws of action are profound and astonishingly accurate. The trader, in either wheat or Steel, could start reasonably close to the bottom of a big advance and follow it **clear through!** One deal would make immense profits and, if pyramided with caution, would make a fortune.

The reader is reminded once more that four out of five bull movements are of the six weeks type and nothing equals the use of the moon phases to forecast the tops of these short term movements. It is, however, of great importance that one should know in the early stages whether the particular movement he is watching is going to run through quickly or drag into a slow bull movement. The slow movement will take months for the uptrend. The quick movement is over with and on the way down in about six weeks. The trader can play the bull side for a full advance, then turn and follow the bear side for a full decline.

BUT YOU MUST KNOW! TO FOLLOW BIG MOVEMENTS THROUGH IS A TRIUMPH OF MARKET SKILL BUT CAN BE ACCOMPLISHED ONLY BY A FULL UNDERSTANDING OF WHAT CONSTITUTES UPTREND AND WHAT CONSTITUTES DOWNTREND.

The information in this course is designed to make the habits and actions of the grain market so clear that the trader may enter and use the market at any of its stages. It is imperative that the successful trader should chart his grain. He should have a chart back for months or a year to see what it has been doing previously. The Grain Trade Review at Kansas City, the Drovers Telegram, also of Kansas City, the Journal of Commerce of Chicago and also the Grain Trade Bulletin of Chicago will have all the quotations desired. Most daily papers have them.

BURIED
TREASURE

The market has its ro-
mance, its deep fascination,
its thrilling stories of
buried treasure. W h o s e
pulse doesn't beat faster at
mystic tales of hidden
wealth? Medieval alchem-
ists spent centuries trying
to change baser metals into
gold. Spanish explorers, in
search of far countries that
would yield more of the
yellow metal, discovered a
new world.

The race has not changed.
Today men bore deeply into
the oil sands of the earth
for the coveted "black gold." They pry mountains apart in search
of auriferous ore. They dig up acres of forlorn, rocky beaches in
search of century-old treasure chests secreted by Captain Kidd or
Black Eagle, famous pirates of the high seas.

Yet men pass thoughtlessly over the shallow hidden "acre of dia-
monds" right at home and from which they could almost kick the
covering dust. More treasure lies buried in the shadow of the big
quotation board than the Spanish buccaneers ever dreamed of.
But always in life treasure goes to the seeker, knowledge to the
student and skill to the one who will practice his art.

Men study the market too lightly and give up too soon. They become frightened or discouraged and turn cynical. They abandon
the search for wealth at the time they should be sharpening their
tools to go deeper. Many a prospector has deserted his claim when
his pick was almost through to the ore. Many an oil drill has been
pulled up when it was just ready to crash through into oil sand.
Success is the most desired thing in the world, but it is an elimi-
nating contest. The one who wins must try and try until he is able
to pass the test. Yet this vast institution, which we term "the
market," is not niggardly of its rewards. It may trample the
thoughtless trader into the dust, but it will pour unbelievable
treasure into the laps of those who will work in sincere harmony
with its laws.

35

The annual wheat crop of North America is worth more than all of the gold mined in the world in a year. And there's more wealth buried thinly under the grim exterior of the old market than lies buried in the whole Rocky Mountain range. Our chief concern is to find the knack of getting it out.

These are not mere empty platitudes. We are talking about real money. A dollar dug out of the market by your intelligence is as good as a dollar dug out of Mother Earth with a plow, a pick or a drill. The market is a business institution, not a crap game, a roulette wheel or a race track. Neither is a man open to criticism because he chances to like the market. One man likes golf, another takes to politics, some devote their lives to bridge and still others bury themselves in their business. If a man's taste calls him to the market he should take the pains to perfect himself in knowledge of the market. Life is too short and time too precious to lose valuable years trying to trick the market out of meager profits by small schemes.

Listen, you men of the world! In your outside business you are shrewd and thoughtful. You plan, you reason, you crush obstacles, you study your business throughout the day and far into the night, you husband your resources, you obey the laws of financial success until you become financial wizards and captains of industry. Why should you not apply those keen wits to the conquering of this willing and munificent market?

Of itself, the market is simple. It is the mirror of men's souls, of their ardent wishes, concealed hopes and their paralyzing fears. Only the human mind is complex. Men are inclined to strangle themselves in a maze of small, unimportant details. The great laws of the market, like the great virtues of men, are very few. They are adequate and cannot be violated. Some psychologist has said "three-fourths of the mistakes are made because a man really does not know the things he thinks he does." Success is largely a matter of concentration, of doing things the right way at the right time. Let your net down on the right side of the boat and it will come up full of fish.

PANNING FOR FREE GOLD

The first mountaineers, who entered the Rockies in search of treasure, had no ore crushers, air drills or blasting powder; they had to pan the soil for its **free gold**. But so prolific was the panning business of "dust" that the Rocky Mountain states were settled by those who sought gold in its simplest form. Later came those who blasted their way into the rocky breast of the earth to lodeŝ and veins of ore and with them came crushing machinery and smelters which take gold from the earth no matter how tightly it may be locked in flintlike quartz.

The amateur can go at his market business in the same way. First, by starting with meager capital—if needs be—and adding to his "dust" until it begins to take on the form of **finances**. It is wise to be satisfied with a moderate return of "free gold" to start with, as there will be lessons to be learned and re-learned as he travels along the market roads. There will be much for him to unlearn. Every trader unfortunately accumulates a "bag of tricks" in his early experience that he finds later are virtually worthless.

The reader of these books shows clearly that he has an unquenchable desire to know his market. It is a compliment to his intelligence that he prefers to get first hand knowledge of the market in which he intends to invest his money. By starting right he can go far.

The experienced operator, with ample capital, will find in these books market laws and methods so amazingly useful that he can begin his next operations with new confidence and can play for stakes greater than he ever thought possible. The smartest market operators are the best students. They are continually in search of vital information. The purchaser of these books should start at the first page and go right through them without jumping over to other books that may seem more interesting. The subject matter has been deevloped progressively, starting with the lesser habits and keys of the market and finishing with the most profound laws known to market action.

THE AMBITIOUS TRADER

The man who will not accept defeat, who knows that back of all this market action there are orderly laws and who studies to learn the proper and safe way to use the market, is the man who will eventually pile up the biggest fortune.

When he had first read this set of books through carefully and was preparing to enter the wheat market he would naturally think that the first step was to go back to the first and second books and, after making careful charts of the principal wheat options he should watch the first, second and third keys for signs of the TREND.

All through the course he has been reading of the high importance of trend and will wish to know whether the market, at the time he is preparing to enter, is in downtrend or uptrend. That's an extremely important point. When he knows the long range direction of the market he has solved half of his difficulties right at the start. He can watch the day to day action of wheat, or if he has the time and facilities he can chart the options back for a year or more to determine when the last bull market top or the last bear market bottom occurred. Then, without waiting, he will know the trend.

If the last big movement made a high, sharp top 25 to 50 cents above the bottom it is a bull market top and from then on until the price is back down to the bottom the market is in absolute down trend. If the most recent big movement was down, then the market is doubtless in gradual uptrend.

He will be extremely fortunate if he finds wheat is at a low position and just emerging from a bottom congestion such as shown in KEY No. 1 of Book II.

And last, but not least, in his plan of operation will be his firm resolve to avoid over-trading as he would a contagious disease. He will not descend to the level of the small talk heard at the exchanges which he knows is nothing more than the further muddling of already muddled minds; in fact, he will avoid the exchange and do his trading by telephone from his desk. Every trade he makes will be kept in orderly fashion in account books and when margins are necessary he will immediately give a check to the broker. Also he will require the broker to give him a check for both profit and margin on each trade as he closes them out. Surplus funds should be kept in a bank, not in the brokerage house.

Our trader will not run to seed on small data. He will not clutter his mind with unimportant details but will concentrate upon the TREND. Bull and bear markets are through movements which are not affected by small events.

He will margin every trade with a grim determination to make it successful. He will develop the art of taking profits, and as his money comes in he will not become careless or over-confident and risk it too lavishly in making new trades. He will understand that capital must not be jeopardized by overworking it or by exposing it in heavy deals. When his funds have increased to handsome proportions he will have increased in judgment and in personal control and will flatly resist the temptation to do big things, but will grow steadily through the years, adding to his increasing revenues and developing his market knowledge to the end that he may reach that cherished goal of all men, FINANCIAL SUCCESS!

THE END

Your Ship is Coming In!

No matter what other things you have to give up, no matter what sacrifices you have to make, let everything else go if necessary, but cling to the ideal which haunts your dreams, for it points to the star of your destiny, and if you follow it you will come out of the darkness into beauty and brightness. Your highest ideal, the vision of your life's work which you long to make real, is your best friend. Keep as close to it as you can, stick to it, and it will lead you to your goal. You may not understand why the star has been put so high above you and why so many mountains of obstacles and difficulties intervene, but if you keep your eye on the star and listen to the voice of your soul which bids you climb on, you will reach it!—Marden.

Recommended Readings

- Riches Are Your Right by Joseph Murphy

- The Money Illusion by Irving Fisher

- How To Win Friends And Influence People: A Condensation From The Book by Dale Carnegie

- How to Make a Fortune Today-Starting from Scratch: Nickerson's New Real Estate Guide by William Nickerson

- How I Trade and Invest in Stocks and Bonds by Richard D. Wyckoff

- The Magic of Believing by Claude M. Bristol

- Scientific Advertising by Claude C. Hopkins

- The Law of Success: Using the Power of Spirit to Create Health, Prosperity, and Happiness by Paramahansa Yogananda

- How I Learned the Secrets of Success in Selling by Frank Bettger

- The W. D. Gann Master Commodity Course: Original Commodity Market Trading Course by W. D. Gann

Available at www.snowballpublishing.com